**UNIVERSITY OF
GLOUCESTERSHIRE**
at Cheltenham and Gloucester

Enga

Case
and R

NORMA**L _nvironm**ent

Edited by Mick Healey and Jane Roberts

**School of Environment
University of Gloucestershire**

Published by:

Geography Discipline Network (GDN)
University of Gloucestershire
Francis Close Hall
Swindon Road
Cheltenham
Gloucestershire UK
GL50 4AZ

First Impression March 2004
Second Impression December 2004

Further copies of this publication are available from this address

Engaging Students in Active Learning:
Case Studies in Geography, Environment and Related Disciplines
ISBN: 1 86174 145 6

Typeset by Michele Hills
Cover design by Trudi James

Printed by:
Severnprint Ltd
Units 8-10, Ashville Industrial Estate
Bristol Road
Gloucester
GL2 5EU

Contents

Part D - Active learning through assessment and evaluation

Foreword

There has been massive interest by central government over the last decade in raising the profile of teaching and learning in UK universities, and in ensuring that what is provided for students is a high quality, cost effective, internationally competitive experience that allows them to realise their potential and launches them into rewarding careers.

The Higher Education Funding Council for England's Teaching and Learning Committee reflected this through policies to encourage coordination and collaboration within and amongst institutions. It wanted to ensure that excellent practice was effectively embedded and disseminated across the sector. To assist this, several high level programmes were initiated – the Fund for the Development of Teaching and Learning (FDTL), the various activities of the Quality Assurance Agency in auditing programmes of study and institutions, the Learning and Teaching Subject Network Centres (LTSN), the Institute for Learning and Teaching in Higher Education (ILTHE), the development of e-Universities UK, and most recently the national competition to identify Centres for Excellence in Teaching and Learning (CETLs). And the profile of Higher Education teaching and learning has undoubtedly been raised, partially counterbalancing the pressures to undertake research.

Whilst all the quality assurance structures can be in place institutionally, and in most UK universities they are, this is no guarantee of a high quality experience for students. Excellence is closely correlated to engagement with research, both subject-related and pedagogic, but we have no proper mechanisms for judging the quality of either the giver or the receiver in Higher Education; much of what matters lies at the level of the individual experience. Excellence depends to a considerable extent on qualities for which we have no metrics: charisma, stimulation, motivation, excitement, curiosity, humour and challenge. Together, these can add up to what colleagues in the School of Environment at the University of Gloucestershire have referred to as the 'magic in the classroom'.

This book contains examples of activities and strategies for actively engaging students mainly at the levels of module, course and teaching session. It cannot be a book of 'spells' but it provides ideas that have been tried, tested and evaluated by staff and students over a number of years. Used by lively and committed staff, these activities appeal to students, allow them to experience some of the challenges of operating in and with the natural, cultural and managed environment, and encourage them to reflect on both the subject matter and their own learning. The subjects cover a diversity of environmentally-related disciplines from pure and applied environmental sciences, through applied humanities disciplines including geography, to subjects associated with the design of new environments. The settings in which they can be used range from e-learning to fieldwork, from laboratory and studio-based activities to the lecture theatre and seminar room.

We hope this book exemplifies both the merits of active learning and how we can strive for excellence with it.

Professor Sir Ron Cooke
Former Chair, HEFCE Learning & Teaching Committee
Chair, Joint Information Systems Committee (JISC)

Carolyn Roberts
Head of the School of Environment, University of Gloucestershire

Introduction
Active Learning and the Swap Shop
Mick Healey and Jane Roberts

Active learning in geography and environmentally-related disciplines is the theme of the 27 case studies in this volume. It developed out of a swap shop held in the School of Environment, University of Gloucestershire in January 2004. Not all staff in the School had been able to participate in the event and those who did participate heard about only a third of the case studies featured in this collection. Therefore, our initial intention was to bring the practices together primarily for sharing internally. However, the excitement engendered by the event and the positive feedback encouraged us to publish the collection and make it available to a wider audience.

Experience of collecting and using case studies for the Geography Discipline Network (http://www.glos.ac.uk/gdn) and the National Subject Centre for Geography, Earth and Environmental Sciences (http://www.gees.ac.uk) suggests that the main interest group will be our colleagues in geography and environmentally-related disciplines. However, many of the ideas, particularly those relating to developing key skills and improving students' assessment performances, are transferable to other disciplines. They are especially useful for illustrating workshops on a range of topics featuring aspects of active learning. Sufficient detail has been included for the reader to see how the ideas have been applied in practice. Contact details of the innovators are given at the end of each case study, so that further information may be sought if it is needed.

Active learning
Active learning is about learning by doing (Gibbs, 1988). It involves a student-focused approach (Prosser & Trigwell, 1999). There is considerable evidence that well-designed active learning is an effective way of student learning (Biggs, 2003; Ramsden, 2003). 'Good practice uses active learning techniques' (Chickering & Gamson, 1987, 3). However, as Ramsden (2003, 113) notes, 'Student activity does not itself imply that learning will take place.' For Gibbs (1988, 9), 'It is not enough just to do, and neither is it enough just to think. Nor is it enough simply to do and think. Learning from experience must involve linking the doing and the thinking.' The theory and practice of active learning in geography and environmentally-

related disciplines has been explored elsewhere by one of the editors of this volume (Healey and Jenkins, 2000; Healey, 2004).

Swap shop

All members of academic staff in the School of Environment were invited to the swap shop, as well as several staff from environmentally-related disciplines in other Schools and the University's Centre for Learning and Teaching. Staff were asked to bring one-side of A4 paper to the session explaining an example of active learning which they practised in their undergraduate or postgraduate teaching (Appendix 1). These were then shared in small groups for the dual purposes of dissemination and peer evaluation. There was about 10 minutes for summarising and discussing each case study. Race's (2001) 'ripple model' of student learning was used as a way to evaluate the practices discussed (Appendix 2). Subsequent electronic discussions refined the ideas to those presented here.

The swap shop proved to be an effective way of engaging staff in discussing and transferring good practices. All the participants who completed feedback forms were positive about the usefulness of the event as an opportunity to share ideas and receive constructive criticism (Table 1). The only negative point raised was that several participants would have liked more time to discuss the ideas.

Table 1. *Positive feedback comments on the swap shop*

- Lively and interesting
- Relaxed and informative, concise presentations which drew out salient features
- Excellent, tight follow up
- Time to listen to colleagues about their teaching and ideas, being creative and positive and then also to discuss and pull in others' experiences
- Excellent idea – repeat at least twice a year
- Ideas to develop my examples
- Enthusiasm, the talent displayed, the level of discussion
- An interesting informative 'low key' but stimulating event
- Discussing ideas with colleagues; taking time out
- Relaxed, interactive

The case studies

The School encompasses an unusually broad range of degree and sub-degree programmes, ranging from environmental science to landscape architecture, and geography to community development. At undergraduate level its modular provision is highly integrated and has been designed to maximise inter-disciplinary synergies and efficiencies (Figure 1, Roberts 2001). Therefore it is perhaps not surprising to find that the case studies mirror this disciplinary breadth. There are also case studies from the tourism and leisure subject area and environmental education. However, the range of pedagogic contexts within which opportunities for active learning have been identified is equally as broad.

Figure 1. Diagram showing integration of modular provision within the School of Environment

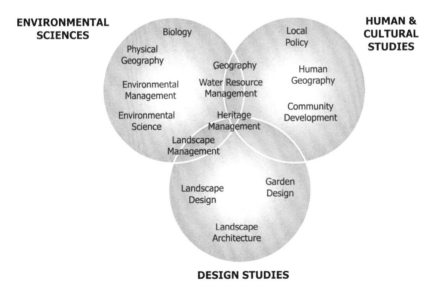

ENVIRONMENTAL
SCIENCES

HUMAN &
CULTURAL
STUDIES

DESIGN STUDIES

Fieldwork, both local and overseas, provides the context for several of the examples. The use of journals to generate, as well as record, reflection (case study C2), or computer generated landforms (case study C4) to develop nascent sketching skills, are imaginative teaching strategies to enhance and extend the active learning opportunities which are inherent in fieldwork.

Structured independent active learning activities (case study A2) also feature here, as does e-learning (case study B5). Learning by doing in voluntary, vocational and pseudo-vocational contexts (case studies A3, C1, C3, C5, C6, C7) stretches the learning experience from the campus to the real world of work, with benefits for students' transferable skills and future career prospects.

But active learning can take place in the classroom, of course. Case study A1 demonstrates how structuration theory can be demonstrated, explained and understood by using video footage of an everyday event in the appropriate pedagogic context. Student-led seminars can lead to deep learning, as well as developing transferable skills (case studies A6, A7). Imaginative classroom based activities can promote student engagement and reflection (case studies A4, A5, A8, A9, B1, B2, B3, B4). Performance in assessment can be improved by interventions which increase students' understanding of assessment process and therefore increase their confidence (case studies D1, D2, D3, D4, D5). Participatory module evaluation simultaneously provides valuable feedback for the teacher and an active learning experience for the student (case study D6).

These examples of active learning are presented here in the spirit of active learning - that is it is hoped that they will be adopted, adapted and applied within geography and environmentally-related disciplines and beyond.

References
Biggs, J. (2003) *Teaching for quality learning*, Buckingham: Society for Research into Higher Education and Open University Press (2nd edition).

Chickering, A.W. and Gamson, Z.F. (1987) 'Seven principles for good practice', *AAHE Bulletin* 39, 3-7.

Gibbs, G. (1988) *Learning by doing: a guide to teaching and learning methods*, London: Further Education Unit. Available:
<http://www.glos.ac.uk/gdn/gibbs/index.htm>

Healey, M. (2004) *Encouraging Active Learning: Applying Kolb's experiential learning theory*, Seminar presented at The Queen's University of Belfast, 28 January

Healey, M. and Jenkins, A. (2000) 'Learning cycles and learning styles: the application of Kolb's experiential learning model in higher education', *Journal of Geography*, 99, 185-195

Kolb, D.A. (1984) *Experiential learning: experience as the source of learning and development*, Englewood Cliffs, New Jersey: Prentice-Hall.

Prosser, M. and Trigwell, K. (1999) *Understanding learning and teaching: the experience of higher education*, Buckingham: Open University Press and Society for Research into Higher Education

Race, P. (2001) *The lecturer's toolkit: A resource for developing learning, teaching and assessment*, London: Kogan Page 2nd edition.

Ramsden, P. (2003) *Learning to teach in higher education*, London: RoutledgeFalmer 2nd edition.

Roberts, C. (2001) 'Mapping the territory at Cheltenham and Gloucester', *Planet, 2,* 15-16

Key words: Swap shop; active learning

Contacts: Mick Healey, School of Environment, University of Gloucestershire; 01242 543364, mhealey@glos.ac.uk

Jane Roberts, School of Environment, University of Gloucestershire; 01242 543279 jroberts@glos.ac.uk

Appendix 1

Organisation of Swap Shop

School of Environment
Active Learning Swap Shop

9th January 2004 09.30-12.00 in TC006

Purpose
The idea of the swap shop is to share interesting teaching, learning and assessment practices associated with active learning[1]. The key question for all participants is 'What aspects of the practices I have learnt about today could I adapt for use in my classes?'

Participation
All teaching staff are encouraged to participate. Please bring 30 copies of your interesting practice. If you are unable to attend on the day, but would like to send in details of an interesting practice, please arrange to let Jane Roberts have 30 copies of your practice by 8th January.

All that is needed is an A4 summary sheet outlining the main features of the practice and how it may be transferable to other colleagues. If you wish to add an appendix giving further details (e.g. the specific task students were asked to undertake) that is optional.

Structure of handouts
The suggested headings to structure your piece are largely taken from the ones used by LTSN-GEES:
- Title
- Name
- Main features - What was the initial prompt/problem? What is the practice trying to achieve? How were your practices changed? What are the gains and losses? What was student feedback? Do you have any other evidence that the activity/practice encouraged student learning?
- Relevant references (where applicable)
- Keywords

Although we would like everyone to bring details of an interesting practice along to swap, if for some reason you have not had time to prepare a handout we would still like you to come along and learn about what your colleagues have been up to in their classes! The idea is to share ideas and reflect on their transferability.

Timetable
09.30 – 09.45   Welcome, context, operation and allocation to groups
09.45 – 10.30   Swap shop I
10.30 – 10.50   Coffee
10.50 – 11.35   Swap shop II
11.35 – 12.00   Plenary: key lessons, publicising the practices, action
                planning and evaluation

Mick Healey and Jane Roberts

Note
[1] Active learning is about learning by doing. It involves an experiential learning student-focused approach and may be contrasted with the transmission model of teaching in which students learn passively. There is considerable evidence that well-designed active learning is a more effective way of student learning than the transmission methods of teaching.

Active learning in environmental disciplines is associated with activities, such as experimentation, studio-based work using real sites, learning in and from work-based activities, problem-based and enquiry-based learning in the field and the classroom, and discussions in-class and on-line. In environmental disciplines active learning is especially common in fieldwork, and laboratory, studio and practical classes, but may be used in all modes of teaching, including lectures. Student-focused uses of ICT are increasing the flexibility of learning.

Evaluating Active Learning Practices

At his workshop on 12th November 2003 on 'Teaching for Active Learning' Phil Race discussed his 'Ripples model' of student learning (Table 1). This focuses on five factors which encourage quality learning – wanting to learn; needing to learn; learning by doing; getting feedback on how learning is going; and making sense of what has been learned (digesting). These five factors provide a possible framework to evaluate the practices we are 'swapping'.

For each of the practices you may like to ask: '***How do the students engage with each of these factors***'? Not all the factors should necessarily be included in every practice. Some will be implicit rather than explicit and some will be covered elsewhere in the course. However, in some cases adding an opportunity for students to engage with the factor explicitly may enhance the quality of the learning.

Table 1: Race's Ripple Model of Student Learning

---

*1 **Wanting to learn:*** How are students motivated/ interested / enthused by this practice?

*2 **Needing to learn:*** Why would they put in some hard work to learn from this practice?

*3 **Learning by doing:*** What are the opportunities for students to practice / learn by mistakes?

*4 **Getting feedback on how learning is going:*** How do students obtain reactions / comments from other people (e.g. students, tutors) about what they have learnt?

*5 **Making sense of what has been learned (digesting):*** What are the opportunities for students to get their heads round what they have learnt?

Based on: Race (2001, Ch 1)

Part A

Active learning on the campus

A1. Using a video of a football match to introduce structuration theory

Andrew Bradley and Tim Hall

Session aims

To use a video recording of a football match to highlight the two major components on structuration theory (structure and agency), to identify the differences between them, and to highlight some weaknesses of this approach.

Time required

15-30 minutes initially with a further 10 minutes to identify weaknesses at the end of the session.

Rationale

- This was developed to demonstrate to students that theories of geography are not merely conceptual and can be seen to be at work in everyday life
- Students 'engage' with theory without realising it, which can help to break down some of their misgivings about the complexity of theory.

Detail of how to implement the session

- The session is not introduced in any way to students. All they are asked to do is to watch the video and to record what happens
- Students watch the video of the football match and write their 'reports'
- Selected students are then asked to read their reports
- What tends to happen is that students record who has done what during the clip
- The session then moves on to given an introduction to structuration theory and its two principal components (structure and agency)
- We then go on to demonstrate how the students' accounts are largely representative of an 'agency' style approach in that they are based on what people do.

- The session then moves on to consider a more 'structural' approach in that in order to understand what is going on we need to consider the 'rules' that govern behaviour.
- Students are then shown the original clip and asked to re-write their report to take account of the rules that govern behaviour.
- The session then moves on to develop in more depth the students understanding of structure and agency and how social scientists have used this theory as a method of understanding human behaviour.
- Towards the end of the session another clip is used to highlight one of the weaknesses of this theory, in that it doesn't take into account human capability in the application of rules. This is done by showing a 'contentious' off-side decision which highlights how it is important to take into account human frailty in the interpretation and application of rules which is something that is lacking from structuration theory.

Linking theory to 'active learning'

- The emphasis here is on getting students to engage with material that many of them will be familiar with on an everyday basis.
- It is through this direct engagement (the report writing/or active learning) that the 'building blocks' of the things they need to know to be able to understand and critique the complexities of structuration theory can be achieved.

Feedback on the session

- This has been very positive from students who have appreciated the use of 'real world' examples to demonstrate complex geographical theories which they feel often have little relevance to the world that they observe around them.

Gains and losses

- Possible that there is some gender bias in the use of football
- Needs to be fully explained beforehand to ensure that students know exactly what is expected of them
- Summary afterwards needs to pay close attention to the relationship between this example and geographical theory in order to create a connection.

Where this example has been used

- *EL323: Society, space and social science.* (Module is an introduction to the theories and philosophies of human geography and the social sciences).

Resources required

- Video recorder
- Video recording of a football game that includes a 'contentious' decision (also helps if the various 'pundits' discuss this decision at some length in the studio after the game!).

Key words: Video; structure; agency; philosophies of geography; structuration theory

Contact: Andrew Bradley, School of Environment, University of Gloucestershire; 01242 543311; abradley@glos.ac.uk

A2. 'In memoriam': preparing obituaries on key geographers

Margaret Harrison

Main features

Society, Space and Social Science is a compulsory human geography module at the University of Gloucestershire. The module aims to place human geography in the wider social sciences as well as provide students with an understanding of the changing nature of geography. Some members of the module teaching team* have research interests in the historical development of geography. To this end staff are eager to illustrate to students how research can and does inform teaching and that some research and literature searches can be fascinating and illuminating.

It is recognised by staff in the School of Environment that many students can find a philosophical module on the development of the discipline both challenging and perceive it as possibly unrelated to other modules they are studying. In an attempt to make the module *Society, Space and Social Science* more attractive and different, the teaching team introduced an 'In memoriam' exercise. The aim of the exercise is to learn about the contribution of one key person to the development of geography. The teaching team believes that by personalising one element of module, content students should gain an understanding of one specific individual, an awareness of context, and an appreciation of the concepts, theories and ideas expounded by the person. The exercise forms part of the summative assessment of the module, and student groups are required to produce one written 'In memoriam' as well as give a brief presentation on the person to the rest of the class. Prior to the introduction of the exercise students received a short series of lectures on the 'founding fathers' of geography; these were criticised for being boring and irrelevant.

The assignment brief for the exercise is to be found in Appendix A2.1. As an exercise in Active Learning students undertake all five aspects of the 'Ripple model' (Race, 2001) in that they are motivated to learn, need to learn, learn by doing, obtain feedback from staff on how learning went and, as a group, make sense of what they have learnt about their particular person.

Gains

- The exercise requires students to work in small groups and has the potential for them to assemble a great deal of material on a particular person;
- Most students enjoy the exercise (evaluation of the exercise confirm this); students become detectives and often explore different angles to obtain information in an attempt to understand their person;
- At best, a group will appreciate how the concepts and theories of one person have influenced other geographers.

Losses

- Some student groups can focus too much on the person and their personal life and thus the 'In memoriam' lacks geographic detail;
- Trying to find accessible literature on some leading geographers can be more difficult than for others;
- Each student will gain expert knowledge on one person but possibly fail to gain an overview of other key geographers.

Overall impression

This exercise does give students an opportunity to study the development of the discipline through the lens of key people. Using the 'In memoriam' idea as an example, students are encouraged to consider and appreciate the role of leading contemporary academics and researchers in shaping the discipline.

* Teaching team normally consists of Iain Robertson, Andrew Bradley, Andrew Charlesworth and Margaret Harrison.

References

Race P. (2001) *The lecturer's toolkit: A practical guide to learning, teaching and assessment,* 2nd edition, London: Kogan Paul

Keywords: Philosophy; historical geography; geographic concepts and theories

Contact: Margaret Harrison, School of Environment, University of
Gloucestershire; 01242 532978; mharrison@glos.ac.uk

Appendix A2.1

ASSESSMENT BRIEF 1

Module code	EL 323
Module title	Society, Space and Social Science
Module tutor	Iain Robertson
Tutor with responsibility for this Assessment (this is your first point of contact)	Margaret Harrison
Assessment	Group oral presentation with supporting text
Weighting	20% of module assessment.
Time limit for assessment	10 minutes oral presentation.
Deadline of submission (your attention is drawn to the penalties for late submission; see UMS Handbook)	The presentation will take place on Week 6. Once the presentation has been delivered each group must submit a typed copy of their 'In memoriam' to the teaching team.
Arrangements for submission	The presentation will take place in the normal lecture room. Written material to be submitted at the end of that day's session with CAMS front cover sheet attached and with group membership clearly stated.

The requirements for the assessment
You will be given the name of **ONE** key person who has 'influenced' the discipline. You are asked to assemble as much knowledge about this person's contribution to Geography and to produce from this information, as a group, an 'In memoriam' article. Each group will then present their work to the rest of the class.

Special instructions
You are advised to make various decisions within your group concerning how you are going to collect information on the person i.e. who does a web search; who explores archival material; who complies the secondary material etc. Please submit evidence of individual group members participation (i.e. who has done what).

Return of work
Within four weeks of submission. To be collected from CL050 during normal opening hours.

Assessment criteria
Quality of factual material including (in particular): awareness of context, assessment of the person's contribution to the development of geography, and evaluation of the concepts, theories and ideas expounded by the person. 75%
Overall structure of the 'In memoriam' article and quality of presentation (Including time keeping and use of visual aids). 25%

The extent to which you have met these criteria is assessed using the School of Environment Grade Descriptors for Level III which can be found in the School Guide.

EL323: Society, Space and Social Science

Groupwork: Key people in the development of Geography: writing an 'In memoriam'

Aim: to learn about the contribution of one key person to the development of geography pre-1945.

Learning outcomes

knowledge and understanding:
On completion of this work students will be able to demonstrate that they can:
- critically assess the contribution of one person to the development of geography;
- have an awareness of context and links to the wider discipline;
- evaluate the concepts, theories and ideas expounded by the person.

Skills:
- synthesise published material from a variety of sources;
- work effectively in a team and produce an agreed document and presentation.

Method
Working in groups, each group will be given the name of **ONE** key person who has 'influenced' and made a major contribution to the discipline of Geography. Groups are asked to assemble as much knowledge about this person as possible in order to **produce and present an obituary for that person**. Each group should consider what aspects of the person's life they wish to emphasise in their 'In memoriam' (in memory of/obituary) but particular consideration <u>must</u> be given to the role of that person in the development of geography as a whole. As part of this you will be expected to discuss the contribution of the person to the development of the discipline both during his (her) lifetime and into the future.

Group members should find information on this person in key Geography texts (both books and journals (for a list to get you started see below)) as well as the Encyclopaedia Britannica and the World Wide Web.

Groups are advised to make various decisions concerning how each member is going to collect information i.e. who does a web search or who explores general archive material, and to keep a log of these decisions, of group meetings and of the amount of work done by each individual member.

Suggested research/organisational methodology (you do not have to follow this) - Everyone reads some examples of obituaries between weeks 3 and 4 (details of 2 obituaries are given below). Meet early to decide who is going to research what and begin this whilst reading obituaries (consult the broadsheet newspapers for additional examples of obituaries). You should then use the session in Week 4 to discuss progress to date, where gaps in knowledge need plugging and a broad outline of the actual presentation. The following two weeks should be allocated to 'fine tuning' your understanding of the life and work (with an emphasis on the latter) and how you are going to present this.

It is critically important that you check early in the research process that there is enough reading available on the person your group is studying. If you have difficulty finding material speak to one of the module tutors.

Each group should keep a record of all individual work undertaken. Remember also to keep precise details of all source material, as we will expect a properly completed bibliography.

Tutors are happy to offer advice on all aspects of your research and presentation but if you do wish to take advantage of this please ensure this is done on an appointment basis.

The presentation
Each group will present their work to the rest of the class in week 6; each presentation should last approximately 10 minutes. Groups may find it useful to produce an OHP, poster or some other visual aid as part of their presentation. Should you wish to use PowerPoint please let a tutor know at least one week beforehand. Once the presentation has been delivered each group must submit a typed copy of their 'In memoriam' to the module teaching team. Attached to the 'In memoriam' should be an outline of the specific contribution of each member of the group to the presentation and written text plus bibliography (including web sites).

Assessment
10 minute orally presented obituary for a key person in the development of Geography (20% of module assessment) and a typed 'In memoriam' article.

Assessment criteria
Quality of factual material including (in particular): awareness of context, assessment of the person's contribution to the development of geography, and evaluation of the concepts, theories and ideas expounded by the person.   75%
Overall structure of the 'In memoriam' article and quality of presentation (Including time keeping and use of visual aids).   25%

Readings
Those readings prefixed by '**S**' are a good place to begin but should not be the only works consulted. You should try to read the original work alongside as much reference material as possible (remember that different commentators will have a different opinion as to the worth of the life and work studied).

Look through the leading Geography journals as these often include appreciations of individual lives and reassessments of key texts.

S - Agnew, J., Livingstone, D. and Rogers, A. (1996) *Human geography: An essential anthology*, Oxford: Blackwell

Barnes, T. and Gregory, D. (1997) *Reading human geography: The poetics and politics of inquiry*, London: Arnold

Bowen, M. (1981) *Empiricism and geographical thought : from Francis Bacon to Alexander von Humboldt*, Cambridge: Cambridge University Press

S – Holloway, S., Rice, S. P. and Valentine, G. (eds) (2003) *Key Concepts in geography*, London: Sage

S - Holt-Jensen, A. (1999) *Geography history and concepts: A students' guide*, 3rd edt., London: Sage

S - Livingstone, D. (1992) *The geographical tradition*, Oxford: Blackwell

Massey, D., Allen, J., and Sarre, P. (eds) (1999) *Human geography today*, Cambridge: Polity Press

S - Peet, R. (1998) *Modern geographical thought*, Oxford: Blackwell

Examples of obituaries

Transactions of Institute of British Geographers Vol. 10 No. 4 1985 pp.504-506: Obituary: Stanley Henry Beaver.

Transactions of Institute of British Geographers Vol. 21 No. 2 1996 pp.429-432: Obituary: Marjorie Sweeting

Key people

Hartshorne	von Humboldt	Ratzel
Mackinder	Ritter	Semple
Herbertson	Davis (WM)	Schaefer
Glacken	Vidal de la Blache	Sauer

A3. The use of a simulated consultancy report as a tool in river/catchment management consultancy training

Lindsey McEwen

Context

This active learning example outlines the changes made to one part of the assessment of learning outcomes associated with a postgraduate taught course entitled *Rivers: Geomorphology and Management*. The module forms an option module within the MSc *Environmental Policy and Management*. Formerly the learning outcomes were assessed using a more traditional, research-based, literature review. While encouraging engagement with the research literature, this did not explicitly develop the students' problem-solving skills, encourage engagement with practitioner literature or allow the development of writing in styles more appropriate to the environmental workplace.

The current teaching and learning approach (involving an individual piece of assessed work) capitalises on the synergies between teaching and research both in individual staff portfolios and more generally among the research group. It encourages active inquiry-based learning through a scholarly approach to teaching (cf. Kolb, 1984; Healey and Jenkins, 2000; Gibbs, 1988).

Aims

The teaching and learning tool aims to get the student to:
- link theoretical scientific knowledge and its application in an environmental policy and management context
- establish the inter-disciplinary nature of catchment management work and the importance of managing land and water together (now particularly important in context of the EU Water Framework Directive)
- engage with the UK and European policy context for different catchment-based environmental problems
- develop research skills, and
- write in different styles for different audiences.

The practice is working to shift the student learning environment to more active learning styles that engender student ownership of a problem-solving context. This is achieved by using teaching and learning processes that simulate research and consultancy processes, thus encouraging a mutually-reinforcing relationship between research and teaching to the mutual benefit of students and staff.

The activity

The teaching and learning method utilises a problem-based approach to active learning. Staff, active in applied research, from within the Geography and Environmental Management Research Unit (GEMRU) of the School of Environment initially establish an applied project brief and problem-identification approach to discussing potential simulated consultancy projects. The student activity revolves around the iterative production of a consultancy report for an imaginary (or real) client which could be an individual or an organisation. In the past, the problem-focus has been geomorphological in character within an environmental management or catchment development context but set in an inter-disciplinary or multi-disciplinary context. In this problem context, the student is asked to select a section of river or a catchment in any region of the United Kingdom, Europe or elsewhere globally.

Practicalities

The report is 3000 words maximum, sectionalised, written in formal report style, word-processed and in a format suitable for presentation in a consultancy meeting. The student is encouraged (with credit given) to integrate relevant diagrams and tables within the text; to help adherence to the word-limit while presenting maximum information. Correspondence with external agencies is included as an appendix.

Assessment criteria involve evidence of the student's ability to:

- display problem identification and solving skills at a level appropriate to Master's study
- evaluate critically the relevance of different investigative approaches and the information they provide
- access different types of literature sources from both pure and applied fluvial geomorphology (pure and applied research literature

and practitioner-led) and to place the problems and issues presented by the selected case study in context
- synthesise information effectively from disparate sources and media
- make valid comparisons (e.g. on the geomorphic impacts of channelisation) with other relevant river sites documented in the research and practitioner literature
- liaise effectively and appropriately with external agencies for data and information
- produce a document in appropriate 'consultancy report' format to an appropriate professional standard.

There are some issues that experience indicates need addressing if the learning format is to work well. These include:

- ensuring that the problem-focus is appropriate for engagement at Master's level
- providing written guidelines as to what production of a consultancy report involves (beyond looking at indicative examples as hardcopy and on the Web)
- supporting anxious students in understanding that information gaps are inevitable and that gap identification is part of the exercise, and
- encouraging students to contact external agencies early in the process to ensure they have time to respond before assessment deadlines.

In addition, there are other logistical and practical factors that influence the success of the learning experience. The project works best as a longitudinal project running through a course, initiated early in course with plenty of development time. Good communication between staff and students is essential. WebCT allows excellent opportunity for shared discussion between students within and distant from the institution (e.g. those undertaking part-time study). It is good practice to offer to review in advance student letters to external agencies to ensure they are well focused and to avoid excessive demands on practitioners. Timely feedback on the initial project proposal is an important determinant in the quality of the final consultancy report.

Some areas of the assessment may still require further construction of support materials e.g. for the development of problem-conception and problem-solving skills.

Evaluation

A number of issues have arisen in the planning and delivery of this active learning format as students need support in developing different skills.

Gains

These are numerous and varied including a more dynamic and unpredictable learning environment that benefits both students and staff (no two projects are the same; there is the opportunity for each student to put their mark on the work). The routine is not the norm - initial ownership of the problem-solving context encourages students to engage and 'want to learn' (cf. Race, 2001). Students 'need to learn' to deliver successfully on the project – encouraging awareness of, and self-reflection on, the learning process is critical to the success of the learning technique. There are other practical benefits in a hectic academic portfolio - student research process may identify useful materials for both student and staff scholarship and further discussion. Very importantly, the more able students are stretched while average students can achieve to the upper range of their abilities.

Losses

The student's engagement with the research literature may be more focused than in the traditional literature review where the synthesis of the research literature is the key element. Engagement with reading around the scientific aspects may not be as extensive for all students. As each project is an individual enterprise, there are time demands on the tutor which would not be there if all students were doing the same project. However, staff-student engagement in the problem-solving activity is normally an enjoyable part of the assessment.

Student feedback

Average student performance is generally improved over the traditional literature review with the most able students frequently scoring at the upper end of the mark range. Comparison with previous modes of assessment has to be made with care, however, as assessment criteria differ. The intensity of student engagement with their self-selected topic and the longitudinal nature of the engagement with the topic and tutor provide two possible explanations for this improvement. Student response has been consistently positive indicating that they found the exercise 'challenging' but 'enjoyable', and that the work integrated well with other aspects of course content. Feedback indicates that students welcome the open-ended, problem-solving approach that allows self-selection of a topic tailored to their own interests and vocational aspirations and the formative approach to project development.

All students in the group are involved in the discussion and negotiation process using WebCT as well as having the opportunity for face-to-face discussion. All therefore gain from both formative and summative stages beyond their own topic and significantly more in the formative stages than in the original literature review. Students also are encouraged to read their peers' reports after they have been marked. As topics selected tend to be very varied in environmental context, the benefits to the student group as a whole in this process are greater than the sum of parts. Later, students have also fed back that they have used the completed assessment as an explicit indication of their problem-solving, synthesis and presentation skills when representing themselves at job interviews.

References

Gibbs, G. (1988) *Learning by doing: A guide to teaching & learning methods*, London: Further Education Unit Available: <http://www.glos.ac.uk/gdn/gibbs/index.htm>

Healey, M. and Jenkins, A. (2000) 'Kolb's experiential learning theory and its application in geography in higher education', *Journal of Geography, 99*, 185-195

Kolb, D. A. (1984) *Experiential learning: Experiences as a source of learning and development,* London: Prentice Hall

Race, P. (2001) *The lecturer's toolkit: A resource for developing learning, teaching and assessment,* London: Kogan Page

Keywords: Consultancy; river catchment; river management; project
               work; problem-based learning; active learning

Contact: Lindsey McEwen, School of Environment, University of
               Gloucestershire; 01242 532970; lmcewen@glos.ac.uk

Appendix A3.1

Further detail on the project

This case study should fall into one of two categories (which are not mutually exclusive).

(a) Scenario 1: The river/ catchment requires a management scheme due to problems, which are broadly geomorphological. These problems might involve some of the following:

- 21st century channel adjustment to historic artificial alteration;
- the geomorphic impact of major floods or geomorphic response to changed magnitude and frequency of the runoff regime;
- downstream channel adjustment to river regulation including damming
- excessive rates of bank erosion in agricultural land;
- sedimentation (e.g. agricultural) leading to implications for biodiversity;
- some exploitative use of the river, such as gravel extraction, having an impact on the quantity and quality of the sediment resource;
- contamination of river sediments through metal mining;
- impacts of urbanisation on hydrological regime and sediment supply.

(b) Scenario 2: The river/ catchment already has a management plan or scheme (e.g. river regulation; channelisation) but there are geomorphic issues as to its effectiveness or ramifications for other sections of river in the same catchment. There may be related ecological issues.

The consultancy report considers the following themes:

Essential items - independent of topic

1.   Outline the nature of the potential (or actual) human alteration to the natural river system at site and/or catchment level (with diagrams as appropriate).

2.   Evaluate the geomorphological implications of the potential (or actual) artificial changes to the river or catchment.
This should include an assessment of:

2.1   The nature and rate of geomorphological change at the selected site or catchment.

2.2   The information needs for effective geomorphological assessment at the site (with reference to what data is available). This could include the data requirements for making a quality assessment (e.g. in terms of sediment transport rates, channel adjustment at different spatial and temporal scales); the methodologies for data collection and broader research design.

2.3   Evidence for the impact of the human intervention on natural (or semi-natural) processes. This should be considered over different spatial (e.g. sediment character and organisation of the channel bed sediments, hydraulic geometry and channel pattern) and temporal scales (e.g. months, years, decades, centuries etc.).

2.4   The advantages and disadvantages of alternative management strategies/ solutions from a geomorphological perspective (and any other relevant perspectives - e.g. hydrological, ecological; riparian or catchment users). The geomorphological assessment should use an appropriate conceptual framework for dealing with geomorphic change that assists understanding of the relationship between process and form on the selected river (e.g. demonstrate understanding of systems, thresholds, equilibrium, sensitivity and timescales of response to external changes, etc.).

Optional as appropriate to the topic:

3.   As a scoping study, the report can evaluate what other areas of expertise would be useful in the planning, implementation and monitoring stages of the artificial channel adjustment.

4.   The report can recommend the procedures, individuals and agencies to be responsible for implementing and monitoring the management scheme.

Students are encouraged to engage with external agencies (e.g. environmental agencies, nature conservation agencies, engineering companies, local authorities) by correspondence or visit in the formulation of the problem, in establishing data availability and requirements and in evaluating potential solutions. A formative process of definition and negotiation takes place with each student through electronic and in-class discussion sessions that benefit both individual and group. Students submit project briefs (2 x A4 sides) outlining the aims of the report, the structure and intended content. Feedback from staff and peers is given on this document so informing the structure and content of the final report.

A4. Discovering the multiple meanings of heritage

Iain Robertson

Introduction

This is a short in-class reading exercise designed to help students recognise the many different ways heritage is understood. It is part of one of my sessions on the Level I module *EL165 Resources*. Normal class size is somewhere between 25 and 40.

The exercise

The session opens with approximately 40/45 minutes of lecturing from me on cultural resources. This concept is difficult to define as, applied in its broadest sense, every natural resource becomes a cultural resource. This does not help students appreciate the utility of the concept. Consequently, we concentrate on heritage landscape as an important and central cultural resource for the way in which it involves the deployment of the past for contemporary purposes. This introductory session, therefore, allows me both to introduce the topic of heritage landscapes as important cultural resources and to suggest to students some of the many different ways heritage can be defined and the implications thereof. At this level and in this introductory session, my main concern is to get students to begin to appreciate the many different definitions of heritage and the purposes to which the heritage can be put.

The next stage of the exercise is to ask students to divide up into groups of 3/4/5, depending on numbers. They are given copies of the glossy magazine 'Heritage' (subtitled 'A celebration of Britain'). This is a magazine produced for both the British and North American markets and it 'celebrates' a very specific form of heritage.

Student groups are asked to take 15/20 minutes working through their magazines identifying:
- the subject matter of the main articles
- the nature and content of the adverts.

I then invite the groups to write up the focus of their main articles on the white board. Feedback takes the form of a subsequent class-based discussion that inevitably comes to a point of recognition that the heritage 'celebrated' is a very narrow form of heritage and that the advertisers are addressing themselves to an equally narrow audience.

Evaluation

I believe this exercise works well but it could be developed further. When I run it again I'd like to give the groups a more diverse range of materials to work with. I'd want to get a couple of groups working with textbook definitions of heritage that contrast with each other and with heritage as defined in the magazine. I'd also want to get other students searching the Internet for definitions of heritage. This would broaden and deepen the discussion and ensure that all students were research active. This is a problem with this exercise especially when the class size reaches its maximum. It is relatively easy for students to remain inactive if they wish, allowing colleagues to look at the magazines and speak for the group.

Provocation

This exercise takes approximately 25/30 minutes to complete, occasionally longer. When undertaking the exercise students are told that the reading takes place over their coffee break. In a 'stand-up and deliver' lecture I normally give students a 15 minute break. This exercise therefore occupies some 10/15 minutes of session time. I believe that I could achieve the same result, via slide illustrations and a graph (all of which could be made available to students) in less than 5 minutes. I worry about the balance between content delivery and this form of active learning. The obvious response to this, of course, is that people rarely admit to having learnt through passive teaching. Nevertheless, as Race (2001) points out, the route to effective learning can begin with face-to-face lectures through the communication and generation of enthusiasm. Nevertheless, I chose not to run this exercise in the current academic year (2003/4) as I felt that I did not have sufficient time available to do so. I would, however, wish to return to this exercise as I think it effective and do not believe in delivering solid blocks of content in monolithic lectures.

References

Race, P. (2001) *The lecturer's toolkit: A resource for developing learning, teaching and assessment,* 2nd edition, London: Kogan Page

Keywords: Heritage landscape; cultural resources; definitions

Contact: Iain Robertson, School of Environment, University of
                  Gloucestershire; 01242 532954; irobertson@glos.ac.uk

A5.   Hazard mitigation practical: Predicting a volcanic eruption

Phil Gravestock

This exercise was designed to help students to understand some of the methods used to predict volcanic eruptions. It simulates the position that a volcanologist might be in while interpreting incomplete data from a range of sources and having to make quick interpretations and decisions. Students are highly motivated and appreciate insights into aspects such as timescales and human issues.

Along with an understanding of some prediction techniques, it introduces a number of important social concepts such as the communication of the threats posed by potential hazards to the local residents, and the evacuation of villages (e.g. How will they be evacuated? Where will they be evacuated? What emergency procedures will need to be put in place?).

General description
The exercise is based around activity reports for four volcanoes, with each group of students tackling a different volcano. When using this exercise with groups containing more than 35-40 students it may be necessary to have different groups assessing the same volcano, although I generally give them different numbers so that it is not obvious that the volcanoes are the same. I have found that the optimum group size is 6-8 students.

The timing of events are based upon real eruptions: volcano 1 is based on the Pinatubo eruption of 1991; volcano 2 on the Krakatau eruption of 1883; volcano 3 on the 1991-1993 eruption at Mount Etna (although in this practical it doesn't erupt); and volcano 4 is based upon a mixture of the Japanese volcano Unzen (1991 pyroclastic flow eruption) and Mount St Helens (1980).

The students are provided with: a hazard zonation map; a list of alert levels and possible indications of the sort of activity that may be associated with each level (from Ewert & Newhall, no date); and a summary chart for recording their decisions. Prior to this exercise, the students will need to have been given information about sulphur dioxide measurements using a correlation spectrometer (COSPEC), gravity measurements, harmonic tremors and gas emissions from volcanic flanks (although these are all at a fairly basic level).

Each group designates one student member who will collect the activity reports. Subsequent reports will only be given on submission of the previous decisions and students should therefore keep a record of the date of the previous report, the alert level, evacuations etc. on the Summary Sheet. It is also important to make sure that the students cannot see how many activity reports are remaining, as this will affect their decision on when the final eruption will take place (it is tempting for the students to interpret some of the precursor activity as leading to an imminent eruption).
In order to maintain 'stress' levels it is useful to put pressure on slower groups – this often leads to hurried, rash decisions.

I have found that common 'errors' are for students to:
- evacuate villages too quickly
- go to a high alert level too quickly
- try to lower the alert level too quickly
- allow people to return to villages when it appears that volcanic activity has decreased.

Consolidating the learning
Possible options for consolidating the learning gained by completing the exercise include:
- Presentations in which the groups outline their decisions and their reasons for their choices. This can then be followed by a self-evaluation of their success, or otherwise, in predicting the eruption, communicating information to the local residents, and evacuating the villages. Other students are encouraged to 'challenge' the group about their decisions.
- Combining two groups to discuss their actions and any revisions they would make in hindsight; this works particularly well if the groups have been working on the same volcano.

The discussions can also include consideration of techniques which may be used to mitigate the effects of volcanic eruptions.

Evaluation

Students often comment that they had not fully appreciated the time-scale involved in the build-up to some eruptions, or the fact that it is not always possible to have all the information required to make an accurate prediction.

Variation

A variation to this exercise is to get the student groups to generate their own hazard zonation maps, prior to providing the activity reports. Some additional information about the nature of each volcano would need to be provided to allow the students to devise reasonable maps.

References

Ewert, J.W. & Newhall, C.N. (no date) *Volcanic crisis in the Philippines: the 1991 eruption of Mount Pinatubo* [online]. Available at <http://vulcan.wr.usgs.gov/Vdap/Responses/Pinatubo91/pina_yrbk-1991.html> (accessed February 2004)

All materials for this exercise can be found at:
<http://www.glos.ac.uk/gdn/abstracts/a3prac.htm>

Key words: Group work; hazard prediction; hazard mitigation; role play

Contact: Phil Gravestock, Centre for Learning and Teaching, University of Gloucestershire; 01242 532790; pgravestock@glos.ac.uk

A6. 'The best way to learn is to teach something yourself': an experiment for teaching fluvial geomorphology

David Milan

This paper describes how students can become active learners through teaching topics themselves to other students. The paper outlines the use of this approach in a Level III undergraduate module in Fluvial Geomorphology, running at the time of writing this article. The idea developed here uses an electronic poster in the form of a Powerpoint presentation (e.g. Whalley and Rea, 1998), as the main teaching resource in the sessions. Race (2000) promotes the idea that one of the best ways of learning is to actually teach something yourself.

Principal objectives

The objectives were to design an assessment based around active learning which:

1) covered a number of different key topic areas

2) gave students confidence in discussing geomorphological issues

3) provided a forum for peer teaching by

    i) encouraging the presenting students to read around their chosen topic

    ii) allowing the class to learn from their colleagues

4) provided an electronic learning resource for future students: the Powerpoint files produced by students were posted into a virtual learning environment (WebCT) which will be accessible during future runs of the module

5) provided ICT skills training in the use of Powerpoint.

Planning and support

The students were put into groups and asked to select a topic. A series of key questions about the topic was given to each group. Support materials in the form of relevant papers and hot links to web sites were posted on WebCT, and a box folder of relevant papers was provided to student groups to encourage them to refer to peer reviewed research articles. The student groups were asked to run a one-hour session on the topic. They were given freedom to run the session as they wished, however they had to use Powerpoint for part of the session. The Powerpoint file would be made available to the external examiner and provide a teaching resource for future students. The success of the students in transferring the subject matter was assessed by a guest member of staff and the module tutor. The group teaching session was worth 20% of the total module mark. Each group was required to submit the Powerpoint file of their teaching session in week 6 of the semester, whilst the teaching sessions themselves ran between weeks 8 and 10. The timing of this assessment was important in order to avoid clashes with dissertation hand-in dates and to allow students to concentrate on another piece of assessment closer to the end of the module.

The assessment brief

Students were asked to work in groups of between three and five to prepare and run a teaching session on one topic from the following:

1) modelling in fluvial geomorphology

- Recent progress in modelling flow and sediment transport
- Progress in aquatic habitat models / ecohydraulic models
- Progress in modelling siltation and fish embryo success in gravel-bed rivers

2) siltation: processes, problems, management issues

3) river restoration and rehabilitation using geomorphological principles

4) impacts of engineering and extractive industries upon channel morphology

5) influence of climate change upon channel morphology

6) dating methods for assessing rates of channel change and incision.

Background details were provided for each topic choice, for example:

1) Modelling in fluvial geomorphology

- Recent progress in modelling flow and sediment transport
- Progress in aquatic habitat and ecohydraulic models
- Progress in modelling siltation and fish embryo success in gravel-bed rivers

The use of models in geomorphology is growing. This has largely been fuelled by increases in computing power and higher quality data. As a group you are given the opportunity to explore how models have been used in fluvial geomorphology. Although you are advised to concentrate on one of the above three areas, you may wish to explore other models which have been used in fluvial geomorphology. There are plenty of recent research articles that discuss the use of two- and three-dimensional hydraulic models such as SSIIM, PHOENICS and FLUENT. Studies using these models have largely focused upon sediment transport, flow structure and morphological development. Aquatic habitat modelling provides a much more applied option. You will need to discuss the PHABSIM model and look at some more recent habitat and ecohydraulic models. Although you will find less published information available on siltation models, there is some excellent information on the SIDO model. This was developed in the US for North American salmon species, however researchers at Southampton University are currently working with the model to adapt it to UK salmonids.

Assessment

The assessment guidelines were published to the students during the first session. They were also discussed with students in the sessions running up to the submission date. In the first year of this assessment it is intended that two staff members assess the teaching sessions and Powerpoint files. An alternative would be to use peer group assessment following the guidelines of Stefani (1994). This may be considered in future years.

Two parts of the session are to be assessed:

1) **Powerpoint file**
- structure
- relevance
- appropriateness of the material used
- evidence of assimilation of ideas and concepts
- reference to published research
- use of illustrations / diagrams / images

2) **Teaching session**
- additional resources provided by student groups
- demonstration of assimilation of ideas and concepts
ability to answer questions.

References

Race, P. (ed.) (1999) *2000 tips for lecturers* London: Kogan Page

Stefani, A.J. (1994) 'Self, peer and group assessment procedures' *in* Sneddon, I. and Kramer, J. (eds) *An enterprising curriculum*, 25-46, Belfast: HMSO

Whalley, W.B. and Rea, B.R. (1998) 'Two examples of the use of "electronic posters"', *Journal of Geography in Higher Education, 22*, 413-417

Keywords: Student-led seminars; fluvial geomorphology

Contact: David Milan, School of Environment, University of Gloucestershire; 01242 532977; dmilan@glos.ac.uk

A7. 'Teaching each other': an example of active learning in a lecture, tutorial or workshop

Mick Healey

The issue

Incorporating active learning into classes is promoted as an effective way for students to learn. There are many devices described in the literature by which interaction between students can be encouraged including, for example, 'brainstorming', buzz groups, and pyramiding. One which is less frequently mentioned, but seems to be effective, is a technique I have called 'teaching each other'. The principle is based on the adage that one of the best ways to learn is to teach someone else.

Application

This idea can be applied when students give mini-lectures or seminar papers, although many students seem more concerned with trying to impress the tutor about their level of knowledge than to teach the rest of the class. In the application described here the context is less formal and involves students working in pairs in which the job of each student is to summarise for the other the main points in a short article or extract that they have read. Each student is given a different section of an article or handout or an extract from two different articles.

I use this technique frequently in a variety of contexts. For example, these include a first year lecture to 150 students examining the break-up of socialism in Eastern Europe (using a Geofile article); a workshop for students on improving their essay writing skills (using the article by Unwin, 1990); and a staff development session on incorporating active learning in lectures (using the workshop handout). I even used it my professorial inaugural lecture, rather to the surprise of some of the audience. These particular exercises lasted between 10 and 20 minutes.

Gains

The main advantages of the technique are that:

- it provides a break in a session in which the students/audience are involved actively in the learning process;
- students absorb more of the material knowing that they will have to summarise it to their partner;
- it can lead in to an informed discussion between the pairs or for the class as a whole.

Hints

For the exercise to work effectively:
- the reading(s) need to be chosen carefully; extracts which give opposing/contrasting views on an issue are good for stimulating discussion;
- the extracts have to be copied and distributed to everyone in advance - this involves a small cost and copyright clearance may be required;
- the purpose of the exercise and the procedures need to be explained (it is useful to put the instructions on an overhead transparency or PowerPoint slide) and the process timed carefully (reminding the audience when they have two minutes left can be helpful); insisting on silence while everyone reads their sections is also beneficial.

Evaluation

Overall the technique provides a useful alternative to covering the same material in a passive lecture format. In 'teaching' a colleague the person undertaking the teaching has to review and reflect on the material they are teaching. This means that they learn this material more effectively than if they are simply listening to someone else tell them. As the participants have the full handout they can always read through the rest of it later if their partner has not taught them very effectively!

Acknowledgement

This case study is a slightly modified version of one which appears on the Geography Discipline Network Resource Database <http://www.glos.ac.uk/gdn/abstracts/a68.htm>

References

Unwin, T. (1990) '2.i or not 2.i? The assessment of undergraduate essays', *Journal of Geography in Higher Education*, 14 (1), 31-38.

Key words: Teaching each other; active learning

Contact: Mick Healey, School of Environment, University of Gloucestershire; 01242 543364; mhealey@glos.ac.uk

A8. Peer group review in design teaching

Nick Robinson

Context

Landscape architecture, along with other design disciplines such as architecture and graphic design, has traditionally used studio critique as a key method of teaching. This technique has provided students with individual guidance and both formative and summative assessment. Studio critique has, in fact, for many years been the most common means of communicating the methods of design practice and of teaching the skills required to implement the principles and theoretical basis of the discipline.

Interactive critique of the kind facilitated by studio critique is necessary at a number of key stages of the development of design solutions. A problem commonly faced by design educators in recent years has been that of ever-higher student to staff ratios and reduced staff contact time. These pressures prevent the allocation of sufficient individual attention to student by the tutor. In general, it is fair to say that such critique of student work is only effective for student to staff ratios up to about 20:1 (depending on the level of study- this is higher at Level I and lower at Levels III and IV).

The ratios encountered in the landscape and garden design modules at the University of Gloucestershire can be routinely 30:1 or more. Staff contact time is a standard 3 hours per week per module for the entire class. Under these circumstances, innovative methods of providing design practice feedback are clearly essential.

Peer review as a learning strategy

In answer to this demand, I have developed a number of practices. The most important is peer group review. This aims to provide students with focused feedback and the chance to present and explain their work and the ideas and research that informs it. These peer reviews also make use of the knowledge and ability that exists within the student group. This knowledge is valuable and diverse because the student group includes postgraduate students with varied first degrees and mature students with work experience, in addition to undergraduate students with their own personal aptitudes and enthusiasms. The review gives students a chance to learn directly from each other under the guidance of the tutor.

Peer review groups are employed to assess and direct their design work at key stages such as the development of a brief, concept proposals and masterplanning. The groups are organised by the tutor to include between 4 and 6 students and to include a range of experience and a variety of interpersonal aptitudes and group-work skills. Group members are required to adopt specific roles including facilitator, presenter (the student presenting and explaining their work), supporter, tester and reporter. These roles are rotated until each member has presented. The time available is then divided between the 4 to 6 students in each group rather than the 30+ students in the whole class.

The roles focus the group members' contributions and ensure a constructive environment. They also encourage genuine critical input. The tutor circulates among the groups and checks on roles and the contribution of individuals as they judge to be appropriate. This process allows students to have a much greater amount of time for both presenting their work at various stages and for review and comment.

In some cases, selected students are asked to present their work to the whole group at the end of the peer reviews. In other cases the main issues to arise in the groups are reported to the whole student group by the student in the reporter role.

The peer group work not only substitutes for traditional interim critiques but also helps to compensate for the reduced studio time and the reduced contact between students in these very large cohorts.

Evaluation

In order to implement these groups I needed to trust that the basic feedback could be provided by students and with less input from myself. It is difficult to make an objective comparison with the traditional critiques. However, the practice has been well received by the great majority of the students that took part.

The benefits of the method have been more student participation and engagement. In particular, students have reported having a greater sense of their own value and having improved confidence in design analysis. It is inevitable that there should be some losses, these have been the reduction in individual contact between students and tutor, and some loss of detailed influence by the tutor on the direction and content of students' work.

Key words: Peer group review; design teaching

Contact: Nick Robinson, School of Environment, University of Gloucestershire; 01242 532923; nrobinson@glos.ac.uk

A9. Three active learning techniques used when working with trainee science teachers

Keith Ross

Technique 1: Learning logs

We encourage students to write learning logs as part of their portfolio of evidence presented for their degree. Box 1 contains examples from final year students reflecting on their own learning of science.

Box 1: *Extracts from graduating students' learning logs*

> 'When I first started my course I was quite sure that classrooms should be quiet places where children got on with their work without chatter. ... My development of an understanding of how children learn science has completely reversed my attitude towards classroom talk. I feel I have developed more in this area of science than any other.'
>
> 'My attitude to science, as well as my subject knowledge, has much improved since I began the course. I realise now that I came with a many misconceptions that were never challenged until I encountered the constructivist approach we used in our own learning at university. I now enjoy teaching science and want to make it enjoyable and meaningful for children.'

Technique 2: 'Tell each other'

This technique is used as part of our interactive lead lectures, which last for 90 minutes and contain many short pauses where students are asked to 'tell each other' their ideas. The technique is used:

(a) for *elicitation* at the start of each part of the lecture where it is followed by feedback and voting to give me an idea of the extent of their alternative frameworks of understanding; and

(b) for *reformulation* which follows my presentation of new ideas and challenges their existing frameworks of belief, where they attempt to verbalise to each other the new way of looking at the world, presented in the lecture. Where controversial issues are introduced, time is given for them to make their own position clear.

The system works this way:

'Tell each other' (talk partners)
This is a powerful technique for asking class questions. When you ask a question you will usually wait for hands to go up. Typically you should wait 10 seconds and then ask someone (not always the ones with their hands raised). Instead, try saying:

'Tell each other what you think makes the bulb light up'
Half the students will have an idea and tell their partner (a few may be off task all together). You then say 'Quiet now, please: hands up those who have an idea' or simply choose people to respond. After hearing each response, you say 'Hands up those who agree?' 'Are there any other ideas?'

In this way every student has the chance to reply. Without this most students know that their ideas cannot be accessed in a big lecture, or even in a group of 20 or 30 students, so they give up, because you are likely to choose someone else. Following the discussion that follows the question, where responses are collected, students can now turn to their partner and nod as if to say 'I knew that, didn't I?' – or else be thankful that their wrong answer remained in their small circle. The students who are asked to reply in open class have had the chance to rehearse their answer (verbally) to their partner, before having to speak it out in class – far more students then become willing to put up their hands to reply.

Many books on learning theory stress the need for 'wait-time' – the books on learning theory say: we tend to accept answers almost immediately, but should give students thinking time of about 10 seconds before accepting answers. The *tell each other* technique is no slower than this wait-time class questioning; yet it involves the whole class. Its value is that it allows (nearly all) students to rehearse their ideas **verbally** before answering in front of the whole class – it really only works if you restrict the time to **10**

seconds. If you give more time it is better to call it group discussion, and you will give them a more structured task.

Student **talk** often needs to come before they write: they must be given the chance to make their own sense of the new ideas in your session. *Tell each other* is the simplest and quickest way to do this.

To summarise:
- It allows you, as a tutor, to find out efficiently and quickly, the prior ideas your students have especially if you use 'tell-each-other – vote' and alert you to possible misconceptions they might have which will undermine the ideas you are sharing with them.
- It allows students to translate what you have said into their own terms allowing them to make coherent notes, rather than copying down someone else's words.

Technique 3: Feedback comments

A numbered tutor comment system is used for providing detailed formative feedback to students (Box 2). Students are required to respond to comments.

Box 2: *Part of a student's concept map & part of list of numbered comments used for student feedback (from Energy unit)*

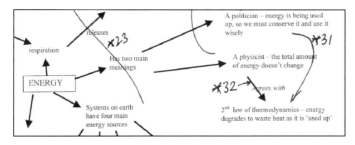

Box 3 shows the assignment with tutor comments and the numbered stars. The extract below is from the feedback sheet given to the students, either when the assignment is set (if the same exercise was used previously) or on return. (For this example only the numbers used in the student extract have been included from the feedback sheet given to all students.)

Box 3: *Example of how the numbered star comments are used by a tutor marking an assignment.*

Results of the elicitation

The children were nearly always focussed on what I was saying during the discussion. I therefore considered this as a sign that it was pitched correctly. The discussion identified that the class knew a force was a push or a pull and could give examples of types of forces. Only one child knew the word 'mass' after much prompting from me. However, the children felt able to (guess the word I was) searching for before this, indicating that I had created a safe environment where children's ideas were valued, which is crucial for effective elicitation (Ollerenshaw & Ritchie, 1997). The written exercise later revealed only two children had been listening to my definition of mass as the 'amount of stuff' in an object (see pp. I and 2, appendix 2). This shows that I had explained it well enough for those of higher ability but perhaps needed to simplify or repeat the definition further for the majority of the class. When asked whether weight was a force and if it would change on the moon the majority of hands went up for the correct option, which was encouraging. The most pleasing result from the discussion was one particular boy who really made the link between weight and gravity and therefore why this would change on the moon. Such unexpected behaviour is an excellent assessment as it gives most insight

*(handwritten margin notes: "S", "*2·4?", "they need time to take ownership of new ideas see *3·1", "or give them time to translate", "are you eliciting or teaching? see *2·4")*

*2 Children's ideas

*2.4   When eliciting children's ideas questions must be asked in a non-threatening way, where the questioner 'genuinely' doesn't know the answer and where the child is 'in control'. See TPS pages P14-16.

*3 Intervention and reformulation

*3.0   Intervention allows the teacher to presents new ideas. Children then need time to make sense of these new ideas which may challenge their existing framework – the reformulation stage of learning.

*3.1   Reformulation (see 3.0) is best done orally. The children need to talk about what they have done and learnt before trying to write or draw.

*3.2   Physicists discovered both the laws so you mustn't say they only agree with one of them. The point is that we are taught the **first law** at school, but not the **second**, which is where the confusion arises.

Keywords: Science education; teacher education; learning logs;
                concept maps; student participation in lectures

Contact: Keith Ross, School of Education, University of
                Gloucestershire; 01242 532802; kross@glos.ac.uk

Part B

Developing key skills through active learning

B1.   Developing students' communication skills

Carolyn Roberts

Context

The School of Environment has as objectives 'to offer students high quality learning, underpinned by successful research and consultancy....', and 'to prepare students for work in a volatile employment area by...developing in students a range of transferable skills...'. In a 2001 survey of advertising for graduate posts by environmentally-related employers (Roberts, 2001) 59% of employers rated 'speaking and negotiating' amongst their top ten skills needs, the highest of any of the specific transferable skills. Moreover, in a wider set of questionnaires, 'speaking to different groups' was highlighted by 75% of environmental employers (again the highest response) and 'advocacy and presenting a case' by 58%. Employers have frequently noted that verbal communication skills are weak in recent graduates, nationally. Actively fostering verbal skills and advocacy hence should be a critical part of higher education for our students, whether on explicitly vocational programmes or not.

Assessment by oral examination

In the areas of hydrology and water resource management, two linked modules *EL269 Hydrological Processes* and *EL372 Managing Water* (and their predecessors) have attempted to remedy this apparent deficiency by focusing students' attention on verbal skills, both through the tuition style and by aligning the assessment method used.

In *Hydrological Processes*, student practicals are structured to develop from the strongly directed, through to the independently designed and implemented, with students being asked to justify their choice of methodology and approach. The module delivery is organised around a workbook, with supporting reading from a set text and research papers, and only limited input from lectures. Assessment of practical work undertaken in field and laboratory settings has been undertaken through structured oral examination, following an interrogative style evidenced in teaching. Practical work covers all the major aspects of the hydrological cycle, from rainfall monitoring, interception and infiltration experiments, soil moisture determination in field and laboratory, to groundwater level monitoring and river flow patterns at the scale of millimetres, bedform, cross-section, reach and basin.

Assessment for the module is 50% oral examination and 50% written examination. Students bring their completed practical notes to the oral, and are questioned on some of their findings for about fifteen minutes. Methodological improvements they might make in their problem solving are explored. As preparation for this, a list of potential topics for discussion is provided in advance, and a 'mock' viva voce examination is conducted in the classroom.

Evaluation

A decade ago, this style of oral examination was regarded with considerable suspicion by students, some academic staff and external examiners. However, the Quality Assurance Agency's Earth Sciences, Environmental Sciences and Environmental Studies Subject Benchmark Statement (QAA 2000) makes explicit reference to the need for students to be able to 'communicate effectively to a variety of audiences in written, verbal and graphical forms', and the style is now more widely accepted. Orals are tape recorded, and written notes kept which are returned to the students to assist them to improve their performance. Students who have completed the module have commented on how useful the oral was in preparing them for job interviews. For tutors, it is easily possible to progress speedily to elicit high quality answers from able and well-prepared candidates, and to highlight weaknesses or gaps in understanding with others. Particularly for weaker students, the immediate feedback is helpful in preparing for the written examination.

Communication through role play

For *Managing Water*, one of the intended learning outcomes is that students can 'distinguish fact from opinion, and present an effective case for particular styles of water resource management'. Another is that they 'are able to work effectively together within a small group'. This is a reflection of the professional domain into which students wishing to work in areas of environmental or water management will move. Early in the module, expression of personal opinion is encouraged through guided seminars using resource materials relating to case studies of conflicting views. Students are cross-examined and required to maintain a case, or at least to speak, in the classroom. Later on, groups of students undertake a role-playing seminar relating to a current issue of water management. Individual students research and act out an agreed perspective, somewhat in the style of a public meeting, inquiry or court case, as they choose. In order to encourage creativity and experimentation, it is not the seminar presentation itself which is assessed, but rather a balanced piece of writing based on their experience with this issue.

Topics such as 'Who is responsible for cleaning up Britain's beaches?', 'Why does Tewkesbury flood?', 'Will there be international water wars in this decade?', 'Water metering is unethical' and 'Should Thames Water be allowed to build a reservoir at Abingdon?' yield sets of relevant stakeholders who can be contacted and interviewed (face-to-face or electronically) prior to the seminar. Positions are selected to be polarised (multi-dimensionally), and the initial adoption of extreme positions is encouraged. As the seminar progresses, discussion usually moves rapidly from cross examination amongst the seminar leaders to wider involvement of the rest of the class. Sometimes the presenters have asked the tutor to act as a Chair or 'Inspector', to manage the meeting; on other occasions a degree of informality has been encouraged, and interchanges have been more anarchic, but always exciting and productive.

Evaluation

Student feedback at the end of the module over the years has been consistently positive about the overall experience, and comments have been made such as 'highly enjoyable'; ...the best thing about the module was 'class participation and use of non-marked presentations'; 'best things were seminars and class participation'; 'interactive discussion, seminars, role-playing... really interesting'; 'seminar preparation, establishing a particular viewpoint, role-playing seminars'; 'the module was interesting and controversial'. Assessed marks have generally been good, and in some cases exceptionally good. It is worth noting that some students find the initial approach rather alarming, but come around to the importance of this skill later on.

Adapting the role-play approach for postgraduate teaching

For postgraduate students, who have been taught concurrently in recent years, the approach is slightly varied, but nevertheless still highly regarded. For these students, a fuller discussion of the role of different styles and purposes of communication may be had, for example drawing on the work of Natale (1997), Hay (2002) and Kontic (2000). The postgraduates then run their own individual participatory seminar, managing information flow from the group, eliciting views and arriving at a shared conclusion or consensus. Frequently, these students are already working in professional areas such as the Environment Agency or water companies, and they are able to develop presentations and enhance their expertise from current work-based projects or interests.

References

Kontic, B. (2000) 'Why are some experts more credible than others?' *Environmental Impact Assessment Review,* 20, 427-434

Hay, I. (2002) *Communicating in geography and the environmental sciences,* 2nd Edition, Oxford: Oxford University Press

Natale, S.M. (ed.) (1997) *Business education and training: A value laden process (Volume 1),* London: University Press of America, Inc.

Quality Assurance Agency (2000) *Benchmark Statement: Earth Sciences, Environmental Sciences and Environmental Studies,* Gloucester: QAA

Roberts, C.R. (2001) 'Skills for environmental employment', Lecture to the Royal Town Planning Institute SW Region AGM, Cheltenham and Gloucester College of HE.

Roberts, C.R. (2002) 'Preaching to the converted? Developing oral communication skills in environmental graduates', *in* Boyle, M. and Smith, Y. (eds), *The International Simulation and Gaming Research Yearbook, 10,* 139-147

Keywords: Transferable skills; communication skills; verbal skills; oral skills; assessment; oral examinations; role-playing

Contact: Carolyn Roberts, School of Environment, University of Gloucestershire, 01242 532922, crroberts@glos.ac.uk

B2.   Building mathematical confidence: DIY continents

Mike Fowler

Background

This 2-hour workshop was originally designed for second year undergraduates at Oxford Brookes University, studying the module 'Biogeochemical Cycles'. The module addresses the short-term (i.e. human timescale) and long-term (i.e. geological timescale) cycling of materials (mainly nutrients and metals) in and between the upper reservoirs of the Earth – the lithosphere, pedosphere, hydrosphere, atmosphere and biosphere. My contribution was to the long-term aspects, and in particular I addressed the long-term evolution of the crust-mantle system, which in short relates to the origin of the continents. This is a profound question as continents are unique to Earth and we'd be a bit stuck and rather wet without them. Ironically, they depend absolutely on water for their existence - 'no water, no continents' is a famous geological quote, though I can't remember who said it first.

More generally, this was one of a number of *numerical workshops* I ran in my courses at Brookes, designed to accomplish two things - one overtly, the other surreptitiously. Overtly, each was designed to help students understand something fundamental about the planet they live on, in this case where the continents came from. Another example was the age of the Earth, which they all ought to know but many didn't. The hidden agenda was to gently remind them that lurking beneath all of the discursive science that we do is *quantification*, which requires that subject they are all frightened of – maths. I remain firmly convinced that a little maths can go a very long way provided we can overcome the initial 'that's maths and therefore I can't do it' reaction. This is easy with well-structured exercises and a relaxed, helpful atmosphere in class.

The exercise

There is one basic diagram which encapsulates the very heart of the discussion surrounding the origin of the continents (Fig. 1) and we can reproduce it from first principles. It involves manipulation of two fundamental scientific equations – for radioactive decay and partial melting. That sounds scary, but isn't when you know how. They all **do** have the required level of maths, but don't like to admit it even to themselves. There is no time to go into detail here, but the workshop is divided into bite-size chunks as follows, each with me leading but them doing (in small groups):

- Calculation of present-day Bulk Earth isotope ratios from known primordial composition using the radioactive decay equation. Draw line 1 on the graph.
- Calculation of parent/daughter elemental ratios in melt and residue produced by a partial melting event using the partial melting equation. Record in a table.
- Calculation of $^{143}Nd/^{144}Nd$ isotope ratio at 3.0Ga. Plot point 2 on line 1.
- Calculate present-day crust (melt) and mantle (residue) isotope values from the calculated parent/daughter ratios in the table, using the radioactive decay equation. Plot points 3 and 4 on the graph and construct lines 5 and 6. Hey presto, job done in **exactly** the same way as in several classic papers.
- You **can** do it, and even if you can't remember the maths, you know it's there and isn't too hard, with a little help from your friends.

Evaluation

As with everything now labelled 'active learning', doing it yourself promotes deeper understanding. The responses received from students when questioned about the exercises during formal module evaluations were invariably positive, and along the lines of 'scary to start with, *but by the end I understood'*. What they actually understood better is one of the most fundamental and unusual properties of our planet, which most folk take for granted.

Use to colleagues

Our students are not good at maths, but we should not therefore ignore it for fear of frightening them. A few examples of hands-on number crunching can be fun, can enhance their understanding and boost their confidence, and crucially remind them of the fundamental nature of science.

Figure 1. Nd Isotope Evolution of the Earth

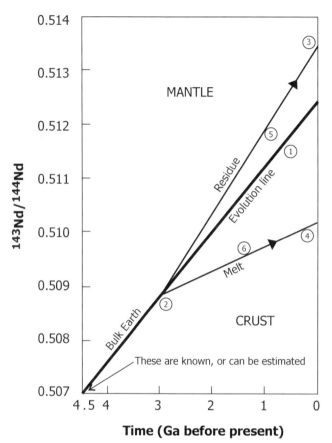

Key words: Numeracy; mathematical skills; biogeochemical cycles; origin of continents

Contact: Mike Fowler, School of Environment, University of Gloucestershire; 01242 543559; mfowler@glos.ac.uk

B3.   Student think tanks: predicting and debating the future

John Buswell

Background

An important aspect of work for some leisure professionals is to predict the future of leisure behaviour and leisure provision in order to plan strategically, make investment decisions and to identify priority needs. A key requirement of this competence is the ability to understand both social trends and product development within the leisure industry and the nature of their iterative relationship. The skills required include the ability to identify appropriate sources of data and to postulate future scenarios of leisure behaviour from various social, cultural political and economic determinants.

Aim

The aim of the session is to link individual work with the processes of group work: analysis, synthesis, and reflective group thinking, as well as organisational skills and time management.

The process

The 'Think Tank' exercise provides the context for the development of these skills through small group work. Students spend time over about six weeks collecting and analysing secondary data and identifying key trends in leisure behaviour and leisure provision and postulating scenarios of future lifestyles and leisure participation. The process culminates in an assessed session in which students present their findings and scenarios, and debate the important issues raised.

This event takes place towards the end of the semester in the module *LM301 Contemporary Issues in Leisure*. Students attend taught lectures throughout the semester discussing various leisure-related issues and topics. They are then asked to form into groups of 4-5 and meet regularly to discuss and debate the issues from the lecture and the given reading. These groups are called 'think tanks' and the purpose of their meeting is to prepare for a presentation and small class debate at the end of semester. The exercise combines various skills:

- cognitive skills with subject-based knowledge and understanding;
- key skills of group work, communication (through presentation and debate) and problem-solving; and
- subject specific skills of forecasting and prediction.

Students are required to refine their ability to discuss and debate at two stages with the need to agree a common position within the small group in the first stage. All individual group meetings are logged and minutes are taken as evidence of meetings taking place outside lecture time.

The assessment

The assessment comprises an individual commentary containing two elements:

a) an analysis of the key issues and their determinants discussed by the group; and

b) a critical review of the influences on their analysis including the group processes and the collective debate.

The main presentation of findings and scenarios takes place in one of the later sessions of the module when the module class is broken down into smaller sub-groups. This is the time the students come together and debate the various issues identified during their meetings. Students should be well prepared and able to enter a lively and topical debate. Issues raised and discussed include the commodification of leisure, the leisure consumerist and participatory dichotomy, leisure and post-modernity, home-based leisure and the relationship between work and leisure.

Student learning

The students are asked to synthesise their analysis of social change with an evaluation of developments in leisure and to consider the implications of their analysis for the role and skills of leisure management.

A key element of active learning also takes place in the second aspect of their written work. Students are asked to reflect on the learning process they have gone through and how their views have changed or been reinforced. They are also required to reflect on the skills learnt and developed and the impact they would have on their role as leisure professionals.

Students have given positive feedback on the exercise. They feel it brings a number of issues together, and their interaction with others and their reflections reinforce and clarify their learning. Students value the knowledge and critical understanding of social and industry trends gained and perceive the skills developed to be invaluable for their leisure practitioner roles.

Key words: Think tanks; group work; debating; forecasting and prediction; leisure

Contact: John Buswell, School of Sport & Leisure, University of Gloucestershire; 01242 543296; jbuswell@glos.ac.uk

B4.   Arguing your case: Development issues in the post-colonial world in the 21st century

Margaret Harrison

Main features

The primary aim is to get students to read, review and reflect on material related to the Postcolonial World and the process of globalisation. An active learning exercise within the module aims to get students to focus on one polarised perspective (positive or negative) of a development topic through the production of a written report. Students work in small groups, or individually, on their chosen topic. All topics have contemporary relevance and in theory should be attractive and interesting to study. Some of the topics that have been studied are Non Government Organisations, the media, multinationals and child labour. The challenge for students is to keep focused on their perspective and, whilst they need to have an awareness of the counter argument, they must emphasise the key development issues for the people and places of the Postcolonial World.

In addition to writing the report, students are asked to give a presentation based on their particular perspective in the same session that the opposing point of view is put across by another student or group. As in a trial, students have to argue their case; an element of competition comes in because both sides wish to win the argument. When not presenting, other students act as the audience and hear all presentations. After the presentations a follow-up discussion occurs in which students outline what they have learnt and how they think presentations could have been improved.

This module is supported by a resource pack (now 2 videos, 2 CDs and a number of key readings) and a short series of introductory lectures on The Postcolonial World. On completion of the initial set of lectures students work independently, or in a small group dependent on module size, on an in-depth investigation of their topic. Students have a meeting with the module tutor to discuss possible sources of material for the topic. At that point the tutor steps back and leaves the students to get on with their work. An electronic discussion forum (WebCT) is available for students to post questions and queries to one another and the module tutor. Engagement with WebCT has been partial; campus based students at Level III tend to rely on face to face communications with one another and the tutor. It will be interesting to observe whether there is greater use of WebCT as more and more students become familiar with it as a means of communication.

Gains

- Students have to conduct tightly focused searches to gain material on their topic and from their allocated perspective;
- Helps students recognise that the same material can be used for both perspectives. What is important is a student's interpretation and reflection, i.e. how does the material support an academic argument from one perspective?
- Presentation helps students to produce clear, coherent reports which emphasise their perspective – in some respects the students are encouraged to think of the presentations as pitting their arguments against the alternative perspective.

Losses

- If students work in a group, inevitably one person may do more work than others;
- Focusing on specific topics can lead students to forget the breadth of study in terms of the overall module;
- Some students can rely too much on web-based sources.

Broader implications for the module

The resource pack took a considerable amount of time and investment by the tutor to create. However, as a result of its use, student learning outside the classroom is now highly structured, resulting in fewer lectures. Students are expected to use the module resource pack extensively. Encouraging students to use WebCT can be difficult when this module has what might be seen as a mixed mode of delivery.

Student feedback

Students find the resource pack to be very good, they value the opportunity to focus in-depth on one topic and undertake research to obtain material to support their argument. Informal feedback after the presentations is that students would like to know whose argument was the best!

Some students use WebCT to discuss their work and enjoy debating the topic with others. The main 'carrot' for this exercise is the fact that the report counts for 50% of the module assessment – so students put in a considerable amount of effort to get a good mark.

Key Words: Independent learning; postcolonial world; globalisation; reflection

Contact: Margaret Harrison, School of Environment, University of Gloucestershire; 01242 532978; mharrison@glos.ac.uk

B5.   Engaging students in active online participation

Elisabeth Skinner

The activity is an online assignment using a virtual learning environment (WebCT) in a cross-disciplinary module *EL102 Management at Work* (Level I, Semester One).

The prompt was the need to engage campus-based students in using WebCT, given an awareness of its benefits as a tool for supporting independent and active learning. The aim is to motivate students to participate and to maintain their involvement so that genuine knowledge construction can occur. It is a bonus that the module content includes the management of people and 'motivation' is a core principle.

The purpose
The activity is designed to help students to
- develop self-management (independent learning) skills
- practise time management
- develop IT skills in general and WebCT skills in particular
- reflect on planned goals
- practise information searching, evaluation and referencing
- exchange information and develop ideas
- experience belonging to an online learning community.

The assignment
The students are expected to demonstrate that they are able to
- make connections between management practice and the literature which discusses management
- identify factors which contribute to the successful management of an individual's progress
- communicate a range of ideas in a professional format
- reflect on their performance.

The instructions

The assignment is offered as one of three options; each option is designed to meet the learning outcomes given above.

'You use WebCT as an online conferencing facility to discuss management in your specific field. WebCT helps you to network with other students who have similar interests, and to exchange information, develop knowledge and reflect on performance. You keep to a programme of small tasks between Week Four and Week Thirteen of the semester. You are assessed on your contributions online - no other submission is required. There are five sessions spread over the semester; each session consists of two tasks. You make a thoughtful contribution to each task and at least one response to someone else's input. Contributions are short and carefully written; you have approximately 200 words per contribution.'

Eighteen students (distance learners and campus-based students) took part in the first run of this activity. They were organised into four online groups according to their subject: the management of heritage, landscape, environment or community.

The five sessions are based on Salmon's five stage model for developing web-conferencing and knowledge construction skills (Salmon 2000).

Stage One	Students begin by gaining **access** to the e-learning site and establishing a **motivation** to participate.
Stage Two	Students engage in **online socialisation** getting a feel for the group or 'community' with whom they will be learning.
Stage Three	Students **exchange information** relevant to their subject and learn from each other.

Stage Four   Students develop their discussion so that they
                        construct knowledge and a greater
                        understanding of their subject.

Stage Five   Students take their **development** further by
                        digesting progress to date and assessing their next
                        steps.

Each session has two tasks as follows.

Session One: Introductions (Access and motivation)

1.1   *Introduce yourself by telling the group four important
           things about yourself. Find a way of helping the group
           to remember who you are.*

1.2   *Introduce your previous experience of management.
           Everyone has experiences of management – at school,
           at work, at home, in the community or in social groups.
           Tell your group about an experience of either good or
           poor management.*

The first task is an ice breaker. It recognises that non-visual clues must be
provided as people get to know each other. These activities reassure
students that their personal experiences are valued and they already have
knowledge that they can contribute (Laurillard 1993).

By asking each student to respond to at least one other student, students
engage actively in what the others are saying and value the
acknowledgement of others.

Session Two: Performance targets (Online socialisation)

> 2.1   What do you hope to learn by doing this assignment and
>   why? What are your strengths and your weaknesses that
>   might affect your performance? Write a short set of goals
>   or targets for this assignment.
>
> 2.2   Motivation provides energy for achieving goals. It is an
>   important management tool. Carry out some book
>   research and find a quote on the value of motivation.
>   Include the quote in your response and provide
>   bibliographic details (see page 9 of the coursebook for
>   how you do this). Then explain why the theory or
>   principles expressed in the quote are useful in
>   understanding management activity.

The students get to know each other in more depth; they carry out active
research and reflect on findings as a group.

Session Three: Information exchange

> 3.1   What are the most important management issues in
>   [heritage] management? There are no wrong answers
>   here so explain what you think the issues are – there are
>   good answers and poor ones however, so think carefully!
>
> 3.2   Recommend one book and one website relevant to the
>   management of activities in your field of study. Explain
>   why each source is relevant and be precise about why
>   you recommend it. Give full bibliographic details for both
>   book and website – see coursebook page 9.

By this stage students have the technical skills and personal confidence
they need for using WebCT and can give full attention to the subject. They
continue to develop information searching skills and to think critically about
what they have found.

Session Four: Management issues (Knowledge construction)

> 4.1   In this activity you extend your discussion in Session Three
>   about management in your field of interest. Your task is to
>   find an appropriate quote in a book about management at
>   work; the quote will be an explanation or definition of a
>   general principle of any management activity. You then
>   explain how this general principle might apply to management
>   in your field of study.
>
> 4.2   What role might an individual play in the management of
>   activities or organisations in your field of interest? Choose a
>   specific role and explain what part they might play and what
>   problems they might face. If you can quote from your reading
>   about management at work, you will get extra credit.

Students continue researching to inform these tasks and reflect on their
findings on the WebCT site. These tasks help students appreciate the value
of comparing theory and practice and develop their understanding further.

Session Five: Performance review (Development)

> 5.1   Before completing this activity, jot down what you think you
>   have learned from this assignment and then reflect on your
>   original goals noted down for Task 2.1. Explain the extent to
>   which your goals have been achieved or not (as the case may
>   be) and note anything unexpected that you learned.
>
> 5.2   Comment on your level of motivation for this assignment. If
>   you were highly motivated, perhaps you could explain why
>   and note whether it helped you to overcome barriers. If it
>   was a struggle to remain motivated, explain why and with
>   what consequences, and suggest how your motivation could
>   have been improved. Again, if you can use a quotation from
>   the management literature to strengthen your points, you will
>   get credit!

Students digest what they have learned and reflect again on key issues of the subject. The task could be more explicit in asking students to review their next steps in relation to self-management, the use of WebCT and their study of management at work.

Gains and losses

The students who chose to undertake this option did not identify any 'losses' but argued that the assignment should be compulsory for all on the module. They developed personal confidence by achieving the aims given above. In particular they noted

- the development of time management and independent learning skills;
- reduction of stress;
- the value of constructive feedback from students and teacher after each task;
- the development of ICT skills involving the new technology of WebCT;
- the value of information searching and clarification of referencing regulations;
- the active sharing of ideas and the benefit of a variety of perspectives;
- the development of skills related to giving support and constructive criticism;
- the realisation through reflection of how much had been learned.

'The support from the rest of the group was really helpful in keeping me motivated. It was good to get feedback from other people, which was always constructive and informative.'

'The point you make about passive and active learning fits well with this assignment - the fact that it has been as much about our own thoughts as those of writers etc and that we have had to make a number of contributions, leading to people responding / questioning our way of looking at management, means we could not sit passively at the screen but had to actively get the computer keyboard working as well.'

Most students maintained a high level of motivation throughout although some found the more pressing need to work on other modules was a demotivating factor. Nevertheless the model contained the flexibility to cope with different commitments and illness. As a teacher, it was pleasing to see the successful outcomes of students' efforts while comments from students demonstrate that the aims of the project had been more than achieved.

Time management was a problem for the teacher, raising questions about scaling up the activity. It was useful to assess the assignment in stages but an initial overspend in marking time was reviewed after the first session. Completed proformas were then attached to the discussion exposing individual feedback to the online group. This proved difficult for some students but in an open discussion the majority of students explained that the process benefited them all.

There was a danger that the teacher would consume too much time responding to individual contributions within discussions so students were warned that there would be feedback only after each two-week session was complete. As fellow students responded effectively to each other this proved an acceptable time management decision. Overall the assignment proved even more successful than originally hoped.

References

Laurillard, D. (1993) *Rethinking university teaching*, London: Routledge

Salmon, G. (2000) *E-Moderating: The key to teaching and learning online*, London: Kogan Page

Keywords: WebCT; learning community; independent learning; reflective learning

Contact: Elisabeth Skinner, School of Environment, University of Gloucestershire; 01242 543275; eskinner@glos.ac.uk

Part C

Active learning in the field and in the workplace

C1. The use of 'live' development sites in the teaching of landscape architecture

Brodie McAllister

Issue

Landscape process-led masterplanning is the setting of development guidelines for a site as directed by natural cycles, for example hydrological cycles. How can students be taught to appreciate the link between theoretical exercises and live operations in this context?

Objectives

a) To use teaching and learning processes which simulate research
b) to give students first hand experience of commercial consultancy
c) to bring data and findings from staff research and consultancy (professional practice) into the curriculum
d) to explore the idea of student project outcomes being determined by negotiation and debate with a real client and publicly accountable agencies, as well as the public themselves.

What does the teacher do?

This particular case study is based on a project taught at third year level on an accredited landscape architecture undergraduate course. The example is based around the main design thesis, taken by approximately thirty students over the whole academic year. Students were asked to produce guidelines for development and a masterplan strategy for Swanscombe Peninsula in the Kent-Thameside area of the Thames Gateway. This is an approximately 10 hectare floodplain, a brownfield site in a strategic government-designated development corridor. The tutor was involved professionally with developers, local authorities, government agencies and co-professionals in neighbouring schemes. The 'real life' problem was the intractable issue of development on a flood plain from an Environment Agency and planning point of view. There was an overlap here in the interests and expertise of the environmental science provision within the School of Environment, and resources available, such as labs and technicians, were drawn upon.

A brief was prepared by the tutor to introduce the project and set out the survey, analysis and design submission requirements, including an emphasis on 3-D visualisation. Other than that, the project was introduced and taught as a joint 'vision' between students, tutor, and concerned parties. This included site visits arranged with prospective developers. The project results were exhibited and assessed at Olympia, London, at the Landscape Industries show. Feedback on the students' work was received from the public, invited Government ministers, and the press, as well as from tutors.

The outcome was an assortment of bold, conceptual ideas that addressed and offered solutions to the problem, in an artistic and environmentally sound way. This benefited the students' portfolios and employment opportunities in a more immediate way than conventional teaching by giving them first hand exposure to commercial consultancy and the economics of development. For example, one student then went on after graduation to work on international competition-winning masterplanning projects at F. Beigel's urban design research unit at London Metropolitan University. It benefited the interested parties (e.g. Environment Agency, developers, locals, the local authority) by proposing solutions that could not be entertained or commissioned easily at a more bureaucratic or commercial level. In addition, it stimulated potential further research opportunities within the School into the relationship between flooding and development patterns (that is, development of large-scale mixed-use schemes combined with public transport). It also brought professional practice techniques and research[1] into a more 'real time' curriculum (one that does not lag behind or predict future planning and development decisions).

The Thames Gateway scheme for immediate expansion and investment in transport and housing provision is one of a number of initiatives involving this and other universities which aim to stimulate a more open, democratic, ideas-led debate on the development patterns of quickly growing regional development areas. The approach has the potential to embed ecological and sustainable principles into the sometimes formulaic developer-led masterplan process, making it a more imaginative, experimental, research-based, and landscape design-driven process.

Context

- Programme: Landscape Architecture
- Module title: Design thesis: regional masterplanning strategy
- Level: 3rd year undergraduate

Does it work?

Evidence that this works is demonstrated by the level of influence of the students on relevant stakeholders, the students' subsequent employability and their positive feedback on this less formal teacher/student relationship.

Problems that have arisen

Although it is a team approach, the responsibility is firmly within the students' domain as to what they want to 'get out of it' - within broad parameters of assessment. This can be very motivating and precipitate hidden potential. Alternatively, it may leave behind those who are confused by a lack of 'spoon feeding'.

Tips

Be aware of students' varying approaches, backgrounds and capabilities.

In the case of this project, the university and students did not enter into a contract with the developer. This avoids potential difficulties associated with expectation and delivery. However, it does mean that the university and students are providing a service that is not paid for directly. There is the opportunity with projects of this type to negotiate costs to cover as a minimum university staff salary and overheads. If successful, this form of consultancy can become a mutually beneficial way of integrating up-to-date professional experience with teaching and bring added income for the university and tutor. In addition, the local community will benefit from increased participation in development debates. Current, ongoing, projects being carried out by the tutor are developing this approach.

Support material

This was in the form of reading lists suggested for landscape architecture generally and urban design in particular; in addition local survey information was in part provided by the tutor to catalyse the process of reaching original design ideas, and avoid students becoming too absorbed in technicalities.

Assessment

Grades were awarded based on achievement set against pre-published
objectives, as judged by presentation to a wide-ranging panel (panel
members included the main developer, other academics, external
consultant urban designers, architects and Architecture Centre
representatives). A group mark was awarded for survey work, and
individual marks for analysis and design. Assessment criteria included: the
fullness of the response to the requirements of the brief; thorough
analysis; thoroughness of execution of an advanced level design; and
communication.

Note
[1] The meaning of 'research' is often defined differently in design fields compared to
conventional science, and usually is a more open-ended process of enquiry and
exploration based around physical spatial problems.

Keywords: Landscape; process-led; joint vision; masterplanning;
                regional development areas; landscape architecture;
                Thames Gateway

Contact: Brodie McAllister, School of Environment, University of
                Gloucestershire; 01242 543280; bmcallister@glos.ac.uk

C2. Self-reflective writing: the use of field journals in studying Holocaust landscapes

Andrew Charlesworth

Context

EL351 Holocaust Landscapes is unique in being a module that teaches about the Holocaust and the heritage of the Holocaust through the study of landscape. It has at its core a five day field class to Poland. The module aims are:

a) to illustrate the post-war representation of the Holocaust in film, memorialisation and museums;

b) to study the landscapes of the Holocaust and the patterns of contestation over such sites in present day Eastern Europe through fieldwork.

Initial problem

When the module was first run in my previous institution a number of students had had problems tackling the formally assessed components of the module, which were a fieldwork project and a formal examination, because they had not had some vehicle of self-expression to articulate and hence deal with their emotional feelings on visiting death camps. One student nearly failed the module because he had not been given the opportunity to express properly his feelings. Getting students to write a daily journal whilst in Poland became the answer and so when validated at this institution the module had such a journal as 50% of the module assessment.

The journal

Learning to write a journal and reflect on one's thoughts and feelings is a crucial skill. Setting up the assessment criteria for the journal in particular is quite difficult. It isn't a question of how much a student writes; it is about the evidence of the degree of reflection as well as the insightfulness of their observations. The journal combines elements of a field notebook which develops the benchmark skills of geographical observation and recording with writing skills that effectively communicate to the reader the self-reflective process students went through as, in this specific case, they contemplated what these sites of evil mean both then and now. The latter relates to subject specific benchmark criteria on effective communication in coursework.

Many of the students in their feedback evaluation in this module have said that writing the journal was the hardest part of the module. This is because expressing themselves in this way is still something unusual for them to do. If they were able to do more of this self-reflective writing then they would be less self-conscious. Certainly in this case giving students the freedom to reflect on their raw encounter with evil allows a greater engagement with the learning aim of the module that states 'students should acquire a more mature understanding of human nature from a contemplation of how ordinary men and women can be so violent to others'.

One way around their reluctance to write in this way is to get the students to begin the journal before they go into the field. By asking them to comment in writing on viewings of video material shown in class or better still watched with others in the class in smaller groups in their own time (with discussion prompts) and on readings given to them, they become both less self conscious and more able to express themselves. Also by having the module tutor read and comment on their first steps in doing such writing they can learn how to do it better and to become comfortable with the experience. I also read the journals whilst we are in Poland and give feedback. Showing past examples of journals can be problematic if excellent ones are shown too early. Students feel cowed that they could never write with such fluency and brilliance. So care needs to be taken when to show them. If ex-students are around it is quite good to get them to come in and reflect on the experience of the module and especially writing their journals.

From my point of view one of the gains from such a self-reflective field notebook is that the module tutor also becomes an active learner on the module. There have been many insights that I have gained from the students' keen and imaginative observations. For example, one student spotted that the depth of soot on the bricks at the top of the archway into Birkenau indicated the number of death trains that had come into the camp. Another student remarked how molehills of ash and bone that can be seen around the camp appeared to be subverting the museum authorities' attempts to tidy up the site through the creation of lawns. Members of the Auschwitz Museum staff are now using the latter observation in presentations on whether their landscape design for the camp is the correct one!

I have tried to get students to share their thoughts with the rest of the class but they are often very reluctant to do so. This is because of the sensitivity of some of the material as just exemplified. Sometimes in confronting issues about death and grief they draw upon grief and tragedy within their own families. They believe that the journals were written for themselves and me and that if they were to be open to a wider audience they would write in a more cautious censored way.

Key words: Holocaust landscapes; reflective journals; field notebooks

Contact: Andrew Charlesworth, School of Environment, University of Gloucestershire; 01242 543349; acharlesworth@glos.ac.uk

ASSESSMENT BRIEF I

Module code	EL351
Module title	Holocaust Landscapes
Module tutor	Andrew Charlesworth
Tutor with responsibility for this Assessment (this is your first point of contact)	*As above*
Assessment	Field Journal /Diary
Weighting	50% of module assessment
Size and/or time limits for assessment	Done as weekly accounts before Poland and on the 6 days in Poland
Deadline of submission (your attention is drawn to the penalties for late submission; see UMS/PMS Handbook)	Monday April 19; for penalties see UMS handbook
Arrangements for submission	School of Environment Office Clegg Building FCH at usual opening times

The requirements for the assessment

Keeping a weekly record before you go to Poland on what you have read and seen. This will be kept to a succinct 200 words per week. In Poland you will keep a daily record which will be, one, field notes of Holocaust landscapes and sites you visit including images and sketches and, two, a record of your thoughts and feelings. There will not be a set daily limit on the number of words you write for that part of your journal.

Special instructions
Samples of previous journals will be available to you. I will read the weekly accounts as you go along and will comment on them and also some of your first daily accounts in Poland. Where you write up the field journal about what you see in Poland, in the field, at the end of each day or when you get back home is a matter of personal preference and rarely affects the grade other things being equal. Thinking about what you see and recording it in an imaginative way and not saying the same thing at every encounter: that is what will decide your grade.

Return of work
I will return personally the assignment and give feedback on the journal. This will be within four weeks from the date of submission at a date and time to be specified and announced to the group.

Assessment criteria
The grade you get for the journal will reflect in part how much you observe and the quality of thought manifested in each entry. This is not a formal writing assignment in the conventional sense but you have to convince the reader that you have looked at the landscape and engaged with it and that you have confronted the issues raised in what you encounter seriously and pondered their implications. That is what an excellent piece does. It makes sense of the landscapes, the places and the people you come across and then 'places' your observations and reflections against a background of material drawn from a wide set of sources some of which can be personal recollections.

C3. Active participation in development: the Kaliro Link Project

Jane Roberts

The Link Project

In 1999 the School of Environment established a link partnership with the National Teachers' College, Kaliro (NTCK), Uganda. The link has two aims:

- to provide opportunities for staff and student development at the two institutions
- to enhance the provision of learning resources at NTCK where this was possible in a cost effective way.

This case study focuses solely on the active learning opportunities for University of Gloucestershire students which have been generated by the link project, although other substantial benefits have been achieved. These include successful staff development experiences for both partner institutions and the transfer of more than forty computers, 3500 books plus other learning resources to National Teachers' College, Kaliro and its partner schools.

Student participation in the link project

Students in the Geography, Environmental Management and other cognate degree and HND programmes have the opportunity to undertake a Field visit to Uganda at Level II to fulfil the compulsory module *EL201 Fieldweek*. Students are invited to choose from a list of possible destinations. The Uganda option is usually oversubscribed and students selected on a first come, first served basis. The group size is about 17 each year.

Normally *EL201* involves a European destination, five or six preparatory sessions, 7-10 days residential fieldwork, plus up to three classroom-based sessions on return. Students opting for the Uganda option, however, are asked to commit to supporting the Link Project, as well as fulfilling the academic outcomes of the module. This they do in two ways:

1. Fundraising. About £2000 is raised by students each year. These monies are not used to subsidise the trip; instead they pay for the export of second-hand books and computer equipment and for the purchase of computer consumables and peripherals for NTCK. In 2002 there was enough money available to pay for two senior NTCK staff to visit the University for three weeks for staff development in information and communication technology (ICT) skills and quality management.

2. Mentoring. Prior to the visit most students undergo a Computer Literacy And Information Technology (CLAIT) or European Computer Driving Licence (ECDL) course in order to develop their confidence in using ICT. During the visit, they offer mentoring to their Ugandan peers in the use of these technologies.

In order to do the mentoring work as well as the academic projects, the trip is 17 days long. For students choosing projects with a Human Geography focus there may be some synergies between Link Project activities and their academic work. For example, past projects have examined the potential gender bias in access to ICT resources at NTCK (and found none). Students whose field of study is more scientific are more likely to undertake projects which have no direct relevance to the Link Project, for example on water quality in townships close to Kaliro or on fisheries management. However, in all cases the quality of learning is greatly enhanced by the advice and local expertise of NTCK academics and the willingness of NTCK students to act as guides and translators.

Evaluation

The Link Project has been an undoubted success in terms of its own aims, with both institutions reporting benefits which are out of proportion to the inputs each has contributed. This approach to curriculum enhancement is particularly appropriate for environmental disciplines but is potentially transferable to students of, for example, education or information technology.

Student evaluation of the trip is very positive, on several levels. Academically, Uganda offers a wealth of active learning opportunities, allowing students to undertake field based project work, in line with the learning outcomes of *EL201*. The opportunity for ICT training, and mentoring is also of benefit, as are the enhanced project management skills associated with organising fundraising events. The opportunity to engage in a prolonged project brings its own benefits - most students' involvement with the Link Project extends over a twelve-month period, in contrast to the usual fifteen-week span of the module. This engenders commitment to the project and enthusiasm for learning.

Student evaluations have also demonstrated that, for a significant proportion of students, participation in the project has resulted in changes in personal attitudes and values. This is not the sort of learning which can be codified as learning outcomes, nor assessed. But it is clear that the Link Project does more than link two institutions. It also manages, for some students, to link the academic curriculum and skills development to changes in individuals' perceptions of the global context of humanity and their own place in this.

Keywords: Fieldwork; Uganda; technology transfer; developing world; key skills; ICT

Contact: Jane Roberts, School of Environment, University of Gloucestershire; 01242 543279; jroberts@glos.ac.uk

C4.   A digital revival of the art of field sketching

Bob Moore

Context

Field sketching is a valuable technique which encourages students to observe, record, contemplate and interpret the landscape. A drawing does not guarantee an accurate record and is highly subjective, but it does have many advantages over photography. There is an extensive literature promoting field sketching in geography, biology and geology at all levels of education. While it is undoubtedly a legacy from pre-photography days, field sketching in these disciplines has provided students of landscape a means of experiencing and interpreting the visual, tangible environment. In his classic book on the subject, Hutchings (1960) claims that 'drawing is something which can be learnt by anyone who cares to study its principles and undertake much practice'. He goes on to list the advantages that sketching has over photography in recording a view, and many are still valid today as supported in the articles of Hawling (1993) and Green (1998) who regard it as a form of field mapping. Annotated sketches are also recommended in landscape character assessments to illustrate 'typical' associations of land elements (Swanwick, 2002).

Photographic technology, however, has now advanced in recent years such that digital images of high quality can be taken by cameras with variable picture formats (including panorama) and even by mobile phones; their success or otherwise can be instantly evaluated in the field. Supplementary information can be recorded using palm-top computers. This is clearly progress, but it rarely achieves the same results of careful landscape scrutiny and understanding which a field sketch produces. It is therefore pleasing to note the research into reviving the dying art of landscape drawing through the development of 'formulated silhouettes' for sketching terrain (Whelan and Visvalingam, 2002). Using computer generated profiles superimposed over high resolution digital elevation models (DEMs), a clearer and simplified (generalised) view of the topography is achieved. This is in part what students in the field aim to achieve through sketching: to observe a complexity of forms, colours and textures and then to make some interpretative drawing of the view. But time spent in the field is always at a premium and a balance must be sought between the time for basic drawing and the inclusion of useful information. Ruskin (1892) talks about 'pure outlines' being a useful shorthand technique when time is limited, and he stresses the importance of 'observance of characteristic points' by careful judgement.

Using digital images to teach field sketching skills

Within the School of Environment, field sketching is taught and assessed in the *EL126 Spatial Data* Level I module as part of a fieldwork component. Formal guidance and even field demonstrations are given, but still some students, who claim limited artistic ability, find the task difficult. The purpose of the proposal outlined in this paper is to encourage such (even all) students to practise sketching using computer technology and to use simplified computer generated three-dimensional views in the field as bases upon which the detail and annotation of sketches can be superimposed. While an artistic gift is clearly an advantage, the argument is that anyone can learn to observe and analyse. It is also hoped that preparatory practice in a virtual landscape will entice students to explore the exciting world of computer graphics.

Using Erdas software, terrain-model perspectives are generated for a number of viewpoints over which geo-referenced aerial photographs or satellite images are draped to simulate the actual scene (sometimes described as virtual GIS). While it is possible to achieve the same effect using photographs taken on site from proven viewpoints, the software allows precise grid references and view angles to be fixed, enabling all the necessary preparation to take place indoors. If students are involved at this stage, it will also develop their basic map reading skills. Once the 3D views are generated (Fig 1), a satellite image or aerial photograph can be draped over the model to achieve a photo-realistic view. This image can be opened in a graphic design program (such as Adobe Photoshop or Jasc PaintShopPro), whereby using the paint command lines are drawn onto a transparent layer to emphasise and simplify the key forms of the topography (Fig 2). Most advocates of field sketching comment that this initial stage of sketching the landscape is the most problematical. Hawling (1993) claims that an economic use of formlines provides the basic framework for the drawing. Such lines determine the proportion and perspective of the view (Moseley, 1992).

Figure 1: *Simple terrain model view*

Figure 2: *Sketching over satellite image drape*

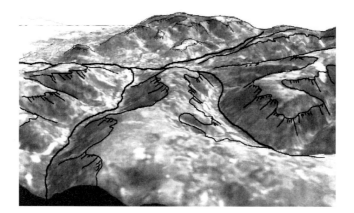

The intention is that the design software can be used as a means to practise such observational and drawing skills, permitting the students to sketch experimentally before venturing into the field. This is not a new idea: tracing paper over photographs is a well-tried technique; even Ruskin recommended it. What is new is the integration of the digital visualisation of landscape with the electronic drawing aids. Once the basic outline of the sketch is completed, additional features can be superimposed (for example, woodland, water, rivers and settlement). Switching off the base layer reveals the 'manual' sketch, on which further enhancements (colour, text annotation) can be made (Fig 3).

Figure 3: *Annotated 'manual' sketch layer*

View looking north

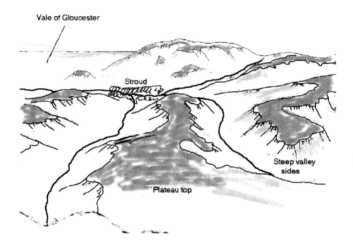

This proposal for active learning in the area of field sketching is currently at a work-in-progress stage and is to be tested in two modules *EL126 Spatial Data* and *EL145 Site Planning*. In both, students will be given the opportunity to practise the identification of key forms and features of a 'complex' landscape and the drawing of them over an authentic base, before applying it in the field. There, it will be possible to provide those students who still encounter difficulties with blank terrain model printouts (eg Fig 1) to sketch over in the field, obviating the problem of initial scaling and proportions.

Evaluation

While I am a keen advocate of traditional field sketching, I believe that this computerised approach to learning the basics of field sketching may be more appreciated by those generally reluctant students who feel they have no aptitude to draw, but who are nonetheless extremely enthusiastic about field study generally, and are able to observe, analyse and more importantly to interpret systematically the landscape. In the best traditions of fieldwork, it will enhance their learning by linking the doing and the thinking (Gibbs, 1988).

References

Gibbs, G. (1988) *Learning by doing: a guide to teaching and learning methods,* London: Further Education Unit. Available at <http://www.glos.ac.uk/gdn/gibbs/index.htm> accessed 23rd February 2004

Green, D. R. (1998) 'Mental mapping and field sketching in geography at the University of Aberdeen', *Cartographic Journal, 35* (1), 83-5.

Hawling, D. (1993) 'Field "sketches": purpose, principles and practice', *Teaching Earth Sciences, 18* (2), 60-2

Hutchings, G. E. (1960) *Landscape drawing,* London: Methuen, 2

Moseley, F. (1992) 'Field sketches', *Teaching Earth Sciences, 17* (2) 61-3

Ruskin, J. (1892) *The elements of drawing,* Orpington: George Allen, 107-17

Swanwick, C. (2002) *Landscape character assessment: guidance for England and Scotland,* Cheltenham: Countryside Agency and Scottish Natural Heritage.

Whelan, J. C. and Visvalingam, M. (2002) *Formulated silhouettes for sketching terrain*, <http://www2.dcs.hull.ac.uk/CISRG/projects/whelan-1/paper.htm> accessed 20th February 2004

Key words: Field sketching; landscape drawing; terrain models; computer 3D visualisation

Contact: Bob Moore, School of Environment, University of Gloucestershire; 01242 532930; rmoore@glos.ac.uk

C5.   The use of group work and presentations on field trips to facilitate active learning

Richard Harper

Issues addressed

This task addresses the following issues;
1. Group interaction and processes
2. Data collection methods
3. Opportunities to reflect on information collected and its usefulness
4. Opportunities to reflect upon the group process of problem solving and personal roles within it
5. Working as a group within a restricted time frame
6. Industry specific task with feedback relating to the industry, task completion and technical aspects of delivering presentations.

Active learning

This task forms 40% of the assessment for the module *TM104 Tourism Field Week*. It is conducted on the last morning of the residential component of the field trip. It requires field-data for its completion, which are to be recorded within a field notebook. The module is formally structured around completion of a workbook and field visits that involve presentations and discussions with local authority tourism officers, site managers, residents and tourists. It requires students to make observations of their own with respect to tourism destination use and management.

The task has been established for Level I tourism management students. It remains fairly formal in terms of guidance but students are encouraged to be proactive in establishing information needs, data gathering strategies and presentation layout and content. The task reflects a typical research question that tourism managers are likely to address within their business environment, and it may appear at later stages within their degree programme where its analysis will occur in significantly great depth than here. Examples of typical tasks might be a destination's relationship with other nearby tourist attractions; issues associated with providing for specific market segments; marketing strategies and the selection of promotional images; the challenges of trying to manage a tourism business in a sustainable way; or tourist perceptions, motivations and satisfactions.

The task represents active learning through two distinct phases:
i)   through addressing the task *per se* which involves problem identification by consensus agreement; collection of information using fieldwork and desk based resources; analysis and synthesis of this information within the context of the problem, and then a presentation to students' peers, tutors and industry representatives.
ii) through an opportunity to reflect upon the processes and learning that may have occurred, which involves students reflecting upon their own ability to collect field data and interpret it; group dynamics and their contribution to these; and their knowledge and understanding of the theory and operations in which the problem was set.

Tasks

*   Student groups are established through a random process of drawing names from a hat. The purpose of this is to reflect industry practice of often working with new or different people, while having additional benefit in helping to break down cliques which may be forming on the field trip.
*   Research topics are posted prior to the residential component to enable students to gather relevant information. Topics are distributed randomly to groups on the first evening of the residential.
*   Students have opportunities to contextualise their topic through the use of a library of resources that accompany the field trip. Concepts are introduced to students within the module's workbook and through informal discussions with tutors.
*   Students are asked to formalise their group meetings and processes.
*   Students are actively encouraged to use primary data from a diversity of sources to address their topic, including their own observations and interview information from the public and industry managers. Within this framework students are directed to appropriate safety and courtesy procedures and the ethical research guidelines that operate across the University. Data collection strategies are established within the group and are supported by tutor approval.
*   Students are advised to meet regularly and tutors monitor group progress.

- Students prepare and perform their presentation on the last morning of the residential, with industry personal present who offer immediate feedback on their findings and their potential application within the sector.
- Within the module workbook students are required to complete a section relating to their personal skills and knowledge development; group processes; both their own and the group's ability to address the topic; and possible improvements they might make in future.
- Feedback is given on a formal module cover sheet, which has a grid that relates specifically to this element of the module's assessment.

Evaluation

The task has evolved to its present state in response to student feedback and staff observations. In particular it is felt necessary that students have time to prepare for the topic prior to their visit. The randomly allocated groups work well in terms of bonding across the student group, although some negative comment occurs from time to time where group members fail to contribute to the task. In general, student comments identify that they enjoy and gain benefit from the applied task and the challenge of a tight time frame in which to prepare and deliver their product; relative 'freedom' to research independently; the fact that they have finished part of their assessment prior to the end of the semester; and the value of 'real' feedback from the industry representative (even if they are daunted by his/her presence).

Tutors have observed positive student development in terms of using theory to inform observation; confidence in field data collection; group work dynamics and group bonding generally; and some lively and novel presentations. Completed sections within the workbook are on the whole completed seriously where students have thought about their own performance and future learning needs, identifying both areas for improvement and some opportunities for this to occur.

Key words: Presentation; group-work; assessment; field-trip

Contact: Richard Harper, School of Sport & Leisure, University of Gloucestershire; 01242 544086, rharper@glos.ac.uk

C6. Live events: active learning through student planned, organised and run events

John Lannon

Context

Many students may have experienced events as a consumer (either at live events or through different forms of media), or through helping to organise an event through schools, tertiary colleges or through voluntary organisations. However the majority of these students have only a 'working knowledge' of event practices due to their roles within these events. This module sets out best practice guidelines for event management and allows students to apply these best practice guidelines through organising, running and evaluating an event situated within the leisure management sector. This paper uses as its framework the 'action-focus model' (Ellis, 1992), which has been identified as ideal for integrating theory with practice and can be used by most professional subject areas, when dealing with practical skills development.

What the module tries to achieve

The module learning objectives are to enable students to:

a) evaluate the growing range and extent of special events and their venues

b) develop knowledge and understanding of the event planning process and utilise this knowledge by applying it to a real event

c) analyse and evaluate the different components involved in organising and running an event

d) undertake the planning and organising of a real event, working in a team situation

e) complete a personal evaluation of their contribution to the event

f) develop a personal skills portfolio based on this evaluation

g) apply numerical techniques to the planning and evaluation of an event

h) observe and give constructive feedback on one other group's event

i) analyse and identify possible problems within the context of an event and propose strategies to minimise associated risks

j) develop group working and independent learning skills.

The events management module attempts to address one of two crucial tests of education that Bentley (1998) identifies, that is the opportunity to allow students to apply what they learn in a practical context. The module assessment is in three stages consisting of the following: a planning document (group based); management of the event (group based); and an evaluation document (individual). This assessment mirrors the action-focus model identified by Ellis (1992) as ideal for integrating theory with practice.

The module allows students the opportunity to follow the stages of managing an event within the leisure industry. The module is delivered by 16 hours of class contact, followed by group and individual tutorials. To provide the students with a purposeful goal (Race and Brown, 1998), a charity is nominated as a beneficiary for all profits obtained. These charities also offer sponsorship in kind (Kotler and Armstrong, 2004) in the form of permission to use brand image, posters stickers, etc. and collection tins. The students are divided into groups of no more than six to undertake the planning and implementation stages. These groups allow students to develop key skills that may not necessarily be practised individually.

These group assessment stages total 60% of the module's assessment. Habeshaw, Gibbs and Habeshaw (1993) identify that group work is problematic and most problems in these instances stem from differential contributions by group members. This can be off-putting for students who may see the group element of the module as a threat to their individual mark. The individual assessment point (the evaluation) was designed so that students have the opportunity (by getting a better grade in this element) to retrieve their individual mark for the module, should their group work necessitate this. The planning document acts as an indicator of progress and is always returned to students at least two weeks prior to their event taking place. The event is then marked by a nominated tutor and students are encouraged to visit this tutor soon after the event to receive feedback that can prove useful to the assessed evaluations.

Evaluation
Student feedback upon completion of the module is very encouraging with all students identifying that the module has met both its learning outcomes and key skills opportunities. They also note that the amount of effort required was more than originally thought. However the majority of students feel that this effort is worthwhile. Furthermore final year students, responding to a current research study by Angela Tomkins, (funded by the

LTSN for Hospitality, Leisure, Sport and Tourism) cite this module as one of the modules that prepares them for the operational demands placed upon them during their placement year (which is scheduled directly after the semester in which the module runs). This has significant implications for their fledgling careers upon graduation.

References

Bentley, T. (1999) *Learning beyond the classroom: education for a changing world*, London: Routledge

Ellis, R. (1992) 'An action-focus curriculum for the interpersonal professions' *in* Barnett, R. (ed.) *Learning to effect*, Buckingham: SRHE and Open University Press

Habeshaw, S., Gibbs, G. and Habeshaw, T. (1993) *53 interesting ways to assess your students*, 3rd ed., Bristol: Technical and Educational Services Ltd.

Kotler, P. and Armstrong, G. (2004) *Principles of marketing*, 10th ed., New Jersey: Pearson Prentice Hall

Race, P. and Brown, S. (1998) *The lecturers toolkit*, London: Kogan Page

Keywords: Integration; theory and practice; skills development; group work

Contact: John Lannon, School of Sport & Leisure, University of Gloucestershire; 01242 522919; jlannon@glos.ac.uk

C7. Reflective thinking on the experiences of work placements

Angela Tomkins

Introduction

This module is designed to enable students, who have undertaken a 48-week period of work experience in the leisure and tourism sectors, to analyse and critically appraise individual experiences, to disseminate information about working practices and procedures in the industry and to become aware of wider issues facing these service sector industries. It addresses key issues such as professional practice and career management and encourages students to reflect on their development of skills and competences and to contextualise their learning within the characteristics and requirements of the leisure and tourism industry.

Two key aims of the module are to:
- conduct an appraisal of placement experiences by providing a forum for the dissemination of information; and
- evaluate personal strengths and challenges identified through placement experiences and conduct a comparative analysis of experiences through discussions and a careers exhibition.

The practice engages students in active learning in two ways. First, it encourages students to reflect on their experiences in industry and, second, they 'learn by doing' in the creation of an exhibition (one of the two assessment methods). About ninety students are normally involved, in 18 to 20 groups, and this provides a 'rich tapestry' of both experience and timely knowledge of those issues affecting the workplace. Students are encouraged to keep minutes of the meetings they hold in relation to the project. As well as being part of the assessed work the information produced is placed in the Industrial Placement Unit for use by pre-placement students.

The industrial experience

Learning starts with the placement and the process students go through. All students will have had the support of an industry-based mentor and a visiting tutor from the university during their placement activities. During the placement period each student will have been required to write a reflective diary which supports the learning they have identified through the four learning contracts they have written. This activity begins the process of personal reflection which is a necessary precursor to the module and the assignments.

The career management assignment

The 'forum' takes the form of a careers exhibition which is assessed in groups of about five and carries 50% of the marks for the module. It addresses three aspects:

(i)   A critical evaluation of the common industry sector including the nature of the organisations and their products and services and how students perceive the sector's key characteristics and trends.

(ii)   A critical reflection of knowledge, skills and personal qualities/competencies required for management in the identified sector, drawing on their personal development

(iii)   An evaluation of potential career opportunities within the sector, including the notion of 'transferable skills'.

The exhibition

Student groups are encouraged to use a range of media to demonstrate their learning on placement and its relationship to career opportunities. Many students choose sophisticated web-based methods, for which there is specialist support, whilst others prefer the more traditional exhibition methods of posters, leaflets etc. The variety of methods used to disseminate information allows students to capitalise on their own strengths and experiences and to appreciate what has been learnt. For example, one group of tourism management students spent much of their industrial placement period promoting the UK on behalf of regional Tourist Boards at overseas exhibitions and were able to bring these skills directly to the assessment situation.

As the exhibition takes place over a half day period, groups of students have the opportunity to look at, and reflect on, work and career opportunities in other sectors – the notion of 'transferability of skills' from one sector to another is frequently reflected in the evaluation of module. When students were asked to identify key learning points on the module, as part of the evaluation of the module, the following comments were made (January 2004):

- How much can be learned from the evaluation of a placement
- Developed my reflective analysis – to be more proactive
- Which qualities are needed to be a professional
- Key resources for future employment
- The value of contacts
- Skills identification -the differences between 'hard' and 'soft' skills
- Career development and 'professionalism'
- The importance of reflection (in relation to learning)
- Learning how to manage time when working in groups
- Continuous Professional Development and the reflective practitioner
- Needing to look back and evaluate what I have done and how this could be improved

Benefits of the exhibition to other students

As well as final year students sharing experiences the careers exhibition is also open to pre-industrial placement students who have a 'first hand' opportunity to speak to individuals about the placements they may be considering for themselves.

Key words: Industrial practice; careers; reflective practice; learning contracts

Contact: Angela Tomkins, School of Sport & Leisure, University of Gloucestershire; 01242 532988; atomkins@glos.ac.uk

Part D

Active learning through assessment and evaluation

D1. Using a self-assessment marking checklist
John Hunt

Context
This paper presents the initial attempts to develop a self-assessment sheet to help students to evaluate their coursework prior to submission. The paper reflects the personal observations of the author arising from over ten years of teaching physical geography and environmental science, and is concerned with an attempt to engage the students to a greater level in becoming self-critical of their coursework during its generation. In essence, this discussion centres on an initiative to encourage reflective learning within an assessment context.

The approach outlined herein has been used in the School of Environment in modules often regarded by the student as being near the 'hard-end' science of physical geography, (e.g. geomorphology & hydrology and Quaternary environmental and climatic change). In particular the approach has been used in the assessment of three modules (Level II *Geomorphology* and Level II *Field-week*; and Level III *Ice Age in Britain*). Underlying the need for this are 3 issues identified amongst the author's teaching colleagues:

- Academics and employers are frequently prone to complain about the declining standards of grammar and expression in the work of students graduating in the higher education sector;
- At the same time, academic and educational guidelines are requiring assessments on degree courses to become better informed by inter-institutional agreement on assessment criteria and grade descriptors;
- Given (i) the pressure on library resources across HE; (ii) the growth of access to non-peer reviewed information on the internet; and (iii) a broad feeling in the national community of external examiners and the teaching team on the specific modules that students often fail to engage with high-end (e.g. research level) literature, staff wished to encourage deeper engagement with library and on-line research journals.

The self assessment form (Appendix D1.I) has been amended from one currently in use by the School of Applied Sciences in the University of Glamorgan (S Jones & A Harris, *pers. comm.*). Whilst the format is designed in light of the points above, sections can be adjusted in order that specific matters can be highlighted. This form serves as the principal feedback opportunity to students at Glamorgan, whereas its deployment at the University of Gloucestershire is in a pilot stage only and is not replacing the established feedback form currently in use across the University.

The Form

An example form is presented in Appendix D1.1. It is broken into six sections (A to F) as follows:

Section A:	Student / Coursework identifiers
Section B:	Checklist for key quality assurance methods (proof reading, presentation factors, adherence to assessment criteria etc.). Students fill in this section and are thereby prompted to act to improve their work.
Section C:	Student / Coursework self-assessment matrix. Students are asked to quality-assess their work based upon 16 criteria, ranking their performance excellent, good, adequate or poor. Whilst the sum of these boxes is not designed to indicate the overall mark for the work, the selected criteria should enhance the students' awareness of what a marker is looking for. These should be filled by the student with regard to assessment criteria and the grade descriptors (Section D). Either here, or on a duplicate (blank form) staff indicate which 'quality rank' they have assigned each criterion. A student can therefore assess where they are over- or underestimating the quality of their work. This should enable improvement in subsequent coursework assignments on other modules. This approach enhances the formative nature of the assessment.
Section D:	Simplified grade descriptors modified from University and School documentation. The students use these qualifiers in completing Section C.
Section E:	This discussion was originally intended for the marker to provide a more holistic / summary comment on the work. Discussions are ongoing as to whether students might use

Section F:
this box as a means of responding to the markers' points within the 'quality' grid (Section C).
Here the marker has the opportunity to highlight major areas for a student to focus on in future coursework.

It should be noted that the form can be adjusted *ad infinitem* by the marking team, to reflect the philosophy and intended outcomes of any particular module or coursework element.

Issues

1. Staff Discussion

The form as presented and the manner in which it has been used, was the subject of intense discussion within one of the School's *fora* on sharing teaching initiatives. Key issues that arose were:

- whether there was a danger that staff would be influenced in the approach to marking the coursework if they had viewed the completed form first. Initial instructions to the student required the form to be placed at the front of the coursework. This has now been changed so that it is the last element of the work, and hence cannot be seen unintentionally by the marker. Staff using the form now complete it only after marking the work. To some degree this reduces staff engagement with the form.

- Whether the marking load would or should be increased or reduced through the use of the form. The form has the capacity to reduce marking time as many issues highlighted by staff in their commentary on coursework are often of a generic nature (grammatical, numerical, graphical) rather than being unique to that essay/report. Tick-box / quality rated feedback (Sections C and F) can reduce the need for the marker to list aspects of the marking as commentary. Therefore, by using the form as an aid to marking, the marking burden could be reduced, leaving greater opportunity to focus on the academic context. However, this would expose the student's self-assessment view to the marker, leading to the potential influence on the marker as discussed above.

  A duplicate, blank form, for the marker's use was highlighted as the solution to this point. However, this could lead to an increased marking load. Additionally, this approach has the potential to disadvantage the weaker and less-engaged student as it dislocates the staff and student response in the quality matrix (Section C). It is questionable whether those students most needy of feedback would decide to combine their responses with those of the marker in order to assess their strengths and weaknesses. This is a perennial problem of feedback. By engaging the student in the self-assessment process it is hoped that a greater interest in the detailed feedback will be engendered.

2. Student Discussion
As the form has only been implemented recently and in a limited number of modules, its impact on quality of performance in written assignments cannot readily be assessed at this stage. As many other factors impinge on overall performance within a module and there are ethical issues that prevent the distribution of the form to a random cohort within a module, it is difficult to see how its benefits can be assessed quantitatively without a properly structured time-series study.

In order to confirm an intuitive sense that the form has beneficial input to the students' coursework psyche, small focus groups were established from students who had been given the form in previous modules. The form's completion rate on the three modules was 28%, 55% and 75%. The focus groups consisted of students who had and had not completed the form. The following points arose:

- Those students who did not complete the form cited ignorance of its existence and time pressures as reasons.
- Of those who completed it, the majority did so at the last point. In completing it these students realised the benefit of the form and would use it sooner if they encounter it in other modules
- All students thought it a positive aid to assignment preparation once they had discussed it.
- Of those students who had used it more than a few days before the assignment deadline, all indicated that it had resulted in a greater awareness of the assessment criteria and of the need to proofread their work.
- Many students who had not completed the form indicated that they did not proof-read their work.

Conclusions

The responses to the initiative have been encouraging. There may be a diversity of approaches in its use by other staff on different modules, but this is not disadvantageous unless it creates confusion in the student body.

From the focus group discussions it is clear that once students understand or have explained to them the context of the form and the potential help it may offer, they are enthusiastic about its role. However, it also seems that this realisation does not become embedded until they have 'missed out' on its use or used it once, but too late for it to exert an influence. In other words, despite staff exhortation, students generally may only develop an appreciation of the value of this approach the second time round. This may point to the benefits of introducing the form to first year students, who may respond more extensively in their second year. In order to ensure its maximum take up, and the early interplay between assignment preparation and the form's role in its improvement, it is recommended that the form is always placed (in hard copy and electronic copy) adjacent to the assignment brief and in the module outline.

Keywords: Self-appraisal; assessment; feedback; quality enhancement

Contact: John Hunt, School of Environment, University of Gloucestershire; 01242 532945; jhunt@glos.ac.uk

When you have completed your assignment, fill THIS form in and place it AT THE BACK of the assignment. Then complete the normal assessment hand in sheet and affix that on top. On this sheet, please tick each criterion in the appropriate box.

SECTION A

Name (optional):	Student Number:
Module Code and Title: EL201 Alpine Project Report	**Submission Deadline:** Monday 17th Nov 2003 15:00 hrs
Assignment Title (summary):	

SECTION B

	4	3	2	1	0
Proof Read (please circle how many times)					

Please indicate that you have checked the:	
Exercise (i.e. is the coursework correctly titled?)	Y/N
Spelling (inc. spell-checking)	Y/N
Punctuation (inc. correct use of apostrophes)	Y/N
Paragraphs (NB: one sentence is not a paragraph)	Y/N
Illustrations (pay attention to referencing and titling)	Y/N
Citations and References (do they correspond?)	Y/N
Assessment Criteria against your coursework (have you done what you are supposed to?)	Y/N
Assignment Brief against your coursework (have you done what you are supposed to?)	Y/N
Presentation (inc. spacing and visual appeal)	Y/N

SECTION C (fill this in after reading the grade descriptors – section D and the assessment criteria in the module guide)

PLEASE ASSESS ASPECTS OF YOUR WORK AS:	EXCELLENT 1st (>70%)	GOOD 2i (60-69%)	ADEQUATE 2ii (50-59%)	POOR 3rd (40-49%)	NOT AT ALL Resubmit/Fail (<40%)
Introduction (effectiveness)					
Context and clarity of problem identification (appropriateness and directness)					
Arguments (coherence, up-to-date?)					
Organisation (is text well organised)					
Illustration (quality of maps, diagrams and graphs)					
Examples or Evidence (quality/number)					
Detail (level achieved)					
Conclusion (quality)					
Titles and Subtitles (appropriateness)					
English (spelling, grammar, punctuation)					
Figures (appropriateness and quality)					
Tables and Plates (quality)					
Paragraphing and Layout (organisation)					
Citations (accuracy / style within text)					
Reference Section (accuracy)					
Reference Usage (minimum threshold – see Assessment Criteria)					
DO YOU CONSIDER YOUR WORK WORTH:	1st (>70%)	2i (60-69%)	2ii (50-59%)	3rd (40-49%)	Resubmit/Fail (<40%)

SECTION D Grade descriptors (modified from University Guidelines)

CLASS	MARK %o₅₀	COMMENTS	MARK AWARDED
1st	70 +	**Excellent** in every way. Analytical, conceptually sound, widely- researched, well-structured. Clear understanding of concepts and principles. Knowledgeable. Read and cited beyond reading list. A degree of flair apparent in the work.	
2i	60-69	**Good to very good**, well-researched, solid. May have some errors in emphasis but not in fact, and may be limited in terms of supporting material and breadth of coverage. Addresses question and defines terms and hypotheses. Sensibly structured. Evidence of analysis and reasoning.	
2ii	50-59	**Average to good**. Reasonable bibliography. May have some errors but balanced by sound work. Signs of effort, though more descriptive than analytical. May not fully address the question or address the topic with deficiencies in knowledge and understanding or directness and organisation.	
3	40-49	**Pass.** Descriptive narrative. May be partly irrelevant. Indiscriminate. Lacks structure. Could be more direct and explicit. Little independent research evident. Short bibliography.	
R (resubmit)	30-39	**Bare pass.** May be confused or irrelevant. Heavily based on lecture notes or without background research, but a minimum of understanding to justify a pass. Answers by inference.	
F (Fail)	0-29	**Poor.** Does not answer question or address topic directly. Little evidence of independent reading or lecture notes. Major errors. Unstructured. Too brief.	
		Very poor indeed. Fails in every respect to answer the question or to address the topic effectively. No evidence of learning, reading or knowledge. Largely irrelevant. Very brief.	

SECTION E

STUDENT COMMENTS:

....
....
....
....
....

SECTION F

STAFF COMMENTS: AREAS TO CONCENTRATE ON NEXT TIME:

English	Spelling	Grammar	Punctuation	Paragraphs/Sentences
Layout	Titles	Subtitles	Blank Spaces	Word-Processing
Illustration	Figures	Tables	Plates	Equations
Technical	Citations	Referencing		
Intellectual	Hypotheses	Scientific context	Link data to discussion	Graph quality

D2.   Use of peer and self assessment to distribute group marks among individual team members: ten years' experience

Mick Healey and Mike Addis

The issue

Group projects are often criticised by both staff and students because frequently when they are assessed team members are credited with identical marks. Although managing the consequences of group responsibility for the outcomes of a project is an important skill which students will often face in later life, giving all members of a group the same mark causes tensions, particularly among the 'better' students who feel their marks may be brought down by less hard working or capable students. One response to this is to use a method for redistributing group marks to allow for the different contributions of team members.

The methods available

The different techniques for identifying the contribution of individuals in project work can be grouped into two basic types. One consists of sharing a pool of marks between team members, the other entails weighting the group mark differently between individuals. The individual weighting factor technique is based on the ratio between the individual score and the average score for all members of the group. This has the advantage of avoiding putting students in the situation where for every additional mark they give to one individual they have to take a mark off another individual.

There is evidence that the latter is a more effective method, in that students are more prepared to allocate a wider range of marks than with the sharing a pool of marks technique (Healey, 1997). Both techniques involve members of the group assessing the relative contribution of team members to the project. The inclusion of a self assessment component raises the mark an individual would have received more often than it lowers it, but the impact is usually small and is offset by the advantage of the feeling of 'fair play' it engenders among many of the students.

Application

The authors have used this technique in a final year module (*EL325 Issues in Environmental Geography*) for the last five years and one of the authors developed the application in the mid-1990s when he was teaching at Coventry University (Healey *et al.*, 1994; 1996). The assessment of the contribution of individuals to group projects is one area of the curriculum in which peer and self assessment are particularly appropriate, because team members are in the best position to judge the quality and effectiveness of the contribution each has made to the project. The use of peer and self assessment techniques help to develop skills of responsibility, autonomy, judgement and self-awareness. Knowing that the group marks will be reallocated to reflect the contribution of individuals helps to discourage the 'freeloader'.

The method in detail

This technique, which is a variant on the technique used by Conway *et al* (1993), awards the group mark to a student who makes an average contribution (Appendix D2.1). Those who make greater (or lesser) contributions receive more (or less) than the original group mark. The method of calculation is described in Appendix D2.2.

Tips

Encouragement needs to be given for students not to simply give all team members the same mark. Emphasising that it is unrealistic that all team members will have contributed equally well to all project processes can help this. Allowing the students to hand in their assessment sheets separately also encourages students to 'tell it as they see it'.

It is sensible to tell the students that if the marks allocated by each student varies widely the tutor may call the group together to explore why. The tutor has the ultimate responsibility for the marks allocated and may on rare occasions need to modify the marks awarded to particular students, for example where there have been breakdowns in personal relationships within the group.

Evaluation

Students are slightly wary of the technique when they are first introduced to it, but are quickly reassured by the fact that: a) the average mark in group work is usually higher than in individually marked work; b) the method allows the different contributions of team members to be taken into account; and c) the self-assessment element enables them to 'tell' the tutor where they feel they have made their contribution.

The technique described here is applicable to identifying the contribution of individuals to group work in any subject and one of the authors has given advice on its application on a range of courses including veterinary medicine, psychology, social work and business studies.

References

Conway, R., Kember, D., Sivah, A., and Wu, M. (1993) 'Peer assessment of an individual's contribution to a group project', *Assessment and Evaluation in Higher Education,* 18, 45-56

Healey, M. (1997) 'Using peer and self assessment for assessing the contribution of individuals to a group project', Geography Discipline Network Resource Database
<http://www.glos.ac.uk/gdn/abstracts/a69.htm>

Healey, M.J., Foster I., Livingstone, I. and Matthews, H. (1994) 'Assessing increasing numbers of students through group projects', *in* Jenkins A. (ed.) 'Teaching large classes in geography: some practical suggestions', *Journal of Geography in Higher Education,* 18 (2), 256-7

Healey, M.J., Matthews, H., Livingstone, I. and Foster I. (1997) 'Learning in small groups in university geography courses: Designing a core module around group projects', *Journal of Geography in Higher Education,* 20, 167-180

Key words: Peer assessment; self assessment; assessing group work

Contacts: Mick Healey, School of Environment, University of Gloucestershire; 01242 543364; mhealey@glos.ac.uk

                 Mike Addis, School of Environment, University of Gloucestershire; 01242 532972; maddis@glos.ac.uk

Peer and self assessment of group project preparation

One of the advantages of working as a member of a team is that you can all benefit from each other's strengths. The purpose of this exercise is to give recognition to the varied contributions that individuals make to the working of a group.

The tutor will use the completed form as a guide to distribute marks between team members. If very large differences occur in the perception of the contribution of particular individuals the tutor may ask the group to discuss these and come to an agreement.

Below is a list of some of the processes which you will be involved in completing a group project. You may modify this list and weightings if everyone in the group is agreed. This is best done near the beginning when you have devised a work plan. You may wish to revise the scheme at the end, but this may result in conflict.

Project processes

> *1 Ideas and suggestions*
> *2 Leadership, group organisation and support, minute taking*
> *3 Data collection/collation/analysis*
> *4 Report writing, production and editing*
> *5 Preparing/giving verbal presentation*

Using the *Self and Peer Assessment Form* independently assess the relative contribution of each team member, including yourself. The following grading system should be applied:

> *1 Minimal, or did not contribute in this way*
> *2 Below average*
> *3 Average*
> *4 Above average*
> *5 Outstanding*

In assessing the relative contributions of team members, account should be taken of the **quality and effectiveness** of the contribution as well as the amount of effort expended.

Average refers to the average contribution of your group members to that particular process.

Self and Peer Assessment Form

Your name:

1   List the names of your team in the table below.

2   Allocate points to each member of your team, including yourself, for each
    project process using the following grading scheme, where average refers to
    the average contribution of members of *your* group to that particular process:
    1 Minimal, or did not contribute in this way
    2 Below average
    3 Average
    4 Above average
    5 Outstanding

3   You are encouraged to use the range of points at your disposal and avoid the
    tendency to give everyone a similar score.

4   Sum the number of points allocated to each person and calculate the overall
    number of points you have given to your team.

Group members in alphabetical order including yourself	Project processes					
	1	2	3	4	5	Total
A						
B						
C						
D						
E						
F						
					Overall total =	

Comments
Use this space if you wish to draw to the attention of the tutor any particular points
about either the way your group operated or the assessment procedures.

Calculation of the score for an individual from the group score using the individual weighting factor technique
(based in part on Conway et al., 1993, p.56)

The example is for a group of three students: Anne, Brenda and Colin. Each student is rated for their contribution by the other two and also assesses her/his own contribution using the grading scale in Appendix D2.1.

Group Members		Project processes					Individual rating
		1	2	3	4	5	
A Anne	A	3	3	4	3	3	
	B	3	2	3	3	3	(42)
	C	2	2	3	3	2	
B Brenda	A	4	4	3	4	5	
	B	4	4	4	4	4	(62)
	C	4	4	4	5	5	
C Colin	A	4	3	3	3	4	
	B	3	3	3	3	3	(49)
	C	4	3	3	4	3	

The individual weighting factor is then calculated from the formula:

Individual weighting factor = individual rating/average rating
Average rating = (42 + 62 + 49)/3 = 51
Anne's weighting = 42/51 = 0.82
Brenda's weighting = 62/51 = 1.22
Colin's weighting = 49/51 = 0.96
Group project mark = 65
Anne's mark = 65 x 0.82 = 53
Brenda's mark = 65 x 1.22 = 79
Colin's mark = 65 x 0.96 = 62

If the deviations from the group mark are thought to differ significantly from the spread of marks found in individual assignments, the individual weighting factor may be scaled up or down. For example, if in the above example the deviations were thought to be too large a scaling factor of 0.5 might be chosen. This would mean that the deviation of the individual weighting factor from the value of one (the weighting for a student with the average rating) would be halved. In the above example, Anne's weighting would then become 0.91 (mark = 59); Brenda's weighting would become 1.11 (mark = 72); and Colin's weighting would become 0.98 (mark = 64).

D3.   Getting to grips with assessment criteria

Jane Roberts

The initial prompt

The stimulus to develop this exercise was the failure of some students in the compulsory Level 1 module *EL101 Environment and Society* to produce work which showed they had taken into account the demands of the assignment brief, especially the assessment criteria. The exercise is designed to make sure that students gave some thought to these, plus the grade descriptors. Rust *et al.* (2003) have undertaken a similar exercise at Oxford Brookes University in the Business School.

The exercise

The exercise involves two hour-long sessions. The class of ninety is split into four tutorial groups each with its own tutor. In session 1, students take part in an exercise about why essay planning in its broadest sense is a good idea. They also work in groups to produce an essay plan for a hypothetical title, then peer-assess this structure. Criteria are not made explicit at this stage beyond 'Will this structure answer the question?'.

They are told to go away and produce an individual plan for the actual title, to the assessment brief. Two weeks later they bring this to the class. The tutor introduces the role of criteria and grade descriptors in assessment. Plans are then clipped to a cover sheet with a nickname (to preserve anonymity), then pooled at the front of the room. In pairs, students review the plans, comparing them against the assessment criteria and grade descriptors and writing comments on the cover sheet. The tutor also reviews some of the plans, and also circulates, encouraging the groups and answering queries. One of the rules is that only constructive comments are allowed. At the end students collect their plans and the comments.

Evaluation

Informal student feedback is broadly positive from the majority.

The exercise clearly increased student awareness of the assessment criteria (Appendix D3.1). However, students found the Grade Descriptors, as currently drafted (see Appendix D3.2) relatively inaccessible. They understand the broad concepts but cannot interpret the descriptors at the detailed level. It is planned to revise them.

Some students do not engage well with session 2, especially those who have not managed to complete the plan beforehand. They spend much of the session developing the plan before joining in.

Reference

Rust, C., Price, M., & O'Donovan, B. (2003) 'Improving students' learning by developing their understanding of assessment criteria and processes', *Assessment and Evaluation in Higher Education*, 28 (2), 147-64

Keywords: Assessment criteria; grade descriptors; formative peer assessment

Contact: Jane Roberts, School of Environment, University of Gloucestershire; 01242 543279; jroberts@glos.ac.uk

Sample EL101 Environment & Society Essay Assessment Brief
[actual title changes for each module presentation]

Assignment 1: Essay (1800 words) (50% of marks for the module)
Submission date: Monday 22 November 1999, at the FCH Faculty Administration Office, between 1.15 and 4.45 pm.

Essay title: 'Examine the extent to which the concept of sustainable development is likely to influence professional work in the field(s) of (X) in the next two decades.'

X represents the major field of study for defined route and major students: joint students may either choose one of their fields or examine both. Students registered on Fields from outside the School of Environment should seek the advice of the module tutor at an early stage.

The essay must be 1800 words (+/- 10% or mark penalties apply) and word-processed with a printed word count.

Assessment criteria
Submissions should:

- be well structured (introduction setting out your approach to the question; paragraphs developing different aspects of the topic in turn; conclusion summing up the arguments).

- be well argued (logical and coherent text making good use of evidence and justifying any assertions made)

- use ideas taught in the module (it is particularly important that you state what you mean by sustainable development and justify your own evaluation of the likely future importance of the concept)

- be referenced using Harvard style (at least 8 different sources required, including Internet, books and journals)

School of Environment Grade Descriptors (see the School Handbook) will be used to assess the extent to which your submission meets these criteria.

University regulations (see UMS Handbook pp. 6-7) on plagiarism (copying the work of others without acknowledging this), syndication (working with other students to the extent that the work submitted is collaborative, not individual) and other unfair means will be strictly applied. This means that, although you are encouraged to discuss your preliminary ideas with other students, the work you submit must be entirely your own. The work will be photocopied and archived as a defence against plagiarism in future semesters. If you allow other students to copy your work you run the risk of the same penalties as if you had done the copying.

School of Environment
Grade Descriptors (Extract only)

LEVEL I

These grade descriptors have been developed to apply to all the diverse forms of assessment used throughout the School. Their purpose is to allow the translation of assessment criteria (which are specific to each assignment) into numerical grades. The descriptors are therefore an important resource for students, as well as for academic staff, as, when read together with assessment criteria, they can help students to understand the qualities which markers are looking for in student work. These descriptors apply to all EL coded modules at Level I.

February 2001

	Intellectual skills	**Key skills**	**Organisational understanding**
A 85%+ Outstanding	All of the qualities in the 70-79 category but at an outstanding level which shows an insight into relatively complex aspects of the subject.	All of the qualities in the 70-79 category but demonstrated to an outstanding level.	All of the qualities in the 70-79 category but demonstrated to an outstanding level.
A 70-84% Excellent	An excellent response to the brief showing a rigorous approach to the acquisition of a broad knowledge base, the evaluation of information, and the planning and development of investigative strategies. Resolution of solutions to a variety of un-predictable problems.	Demonstrates excellent communication skills. Evidence of the selective use of a good range of information sources, correctly cited and, to some extent, independently researched.	The work shows good under-standing of some aspects of the institutional context. Work shows good team working skills.
B 60-69% Good	A good response to the brief showing a rigorous approach to the acquisition of a broad knowledge base, the evaluation of information, and the planning and development of investigative strategies. Development of solutions to a variety of unpredictable problems.	Demonstrates a satisfactory ability to communicate information. Use of an appropriate range of information sources, referenced correctly.	The influence of some aspects of the institutional context is recognised. Work shows satisfactory team working skills.

C 50-59% **Satisfactory**	A satisfactory response to the brief showing a rigorous approach to the acquisition of a broad knowledge base, the evaluation of information, and the planning and development of investigative strategies. Development of solutions to a variety of unpredictable problems.	Satisfactory ability in verbal/written/ visual presentation. Use of a limited range of information sources, referencing largely correct.	Basic acknowledge- ment of some aspects of the institutional context. Basic ability to work as part of a team.
D 40-49% **Adequate**	Basic and/or partial approach to the acquisition of a broad knowledge base, the evaluation of information, and the planning and development of investigative strategies. Consideration of solutions to a variety of unpredictable problems.	Limited evidence of ability in verbal/written/ visual presentation. Narrow or not wholly appropriate range of information sources, referencing used but some errors.	Limited acknowledge- ment of some aspects of the institutional context. Limited ability to work as part of a team.
R 30-39% **Un-** **satisfactory** **but capable** **of being** **brought up** **to pass** **standard**	Some attempt has been made to demonstrate the acquisition of a broad knowledge base, the evaluation of information, and the planning and development of investigative strategies, but this is an inadequate response to the brief.	Communication of information through written/verbal/visual means is inadequate. References inadequate in scope and depth, poor citation.	Little acknowledge- ment or awareness of institutional context. Little evidence of ability to work as part of a team.
F 20-29% **Un-** **satisfactory** **and** **incapable of** **being** **brought up** **to pass** **standard**	Failure to appreciate the key elements of the brief. Inadequate approach to the acquisition of a broad knowledge base, the evaluation of information, and the planning and development of investigative strategies.	Very poor commun- ication skills shown. Inappropriate or inadequate use of sources; little use of information sources, poor or no citations. little or no use of references.	No acknowledge- ment or awareness of institutional context. No evidence of ability to work as part of a team.
F 1- 19% **Fail**	Very inadequate response, showing little evidence of even basic understanding of the task and/or the subject.	Basic communication by written/verbal/ visual means has not been achieved. Minimal research and background reading.	No acknowledge- ment or awareness of institutional context. No evidence of ability to work as part of a team.
F 0%	non-submission	non-submission	non-submission

D4. Active learning techniques to improve student preparation for and performance in examinations: results from a five year trial

Christopher Short

Issue discussed with students

A common issue across a wide range of modules was that students appeared to perform consistently less well in examinations when compared to coursework. As module tutor of a Level II module, *EL208 Managing the Rural Environment*, with two elements both worth 50%, an examination and a consultancy report, I spent some time exploring with the students the possible reasons behind this imbalance in performance.

Results of discussions with students

From these discussions it appeared that the students identified two separate issues that were linked to consistent poor performance in examinations.

First, students felt that lecture notes and associated material, and therefore implicitly the manner in which lectures were delivered, did not provide a sufficiently tangible link with the examination assessment. By comparison, the links with the coursework were more evident and more time was spent in the lectures explaining what was required in the coursework.

Second, the students felt inadequately prepared for the key processes of determining and delivering a response to the examination questions. For some students it would appear that examination questions almost become like a cryptic crossword clue. The only explicit preparation for students on some but not all modules with examinations was a revision session available at the end of the module.

Action taken

The aim of this activity was to find ways of improving a student's preparation for and understanding of examinations and examination questions. Two techniques were tested on the students.

Approach One

First, in response to lack of a tangible link between lecture material and examinations an 'Additional Study' sheet was prepared for each of the main sessions within the module. This contained the learning outcomes of that particular session, two pieces of additional study, relevant references and two examination questions from previous examination papers that were linked to this topic (Appendix D4.1). The aim of this is to provide the students with the means by which to assess their own learning and a mechanism by which they can digest the areas covered. This can be undertaken in the same week as the lecture(s) or during a revision period. The study sheet is always introduced and discussed during the lecture. In the example detailed in Appendix D4.1 abstracts from four relevant journal articles are included in addition. These are discussed in class to encourage engagement with journal articles but also in terms of some of the barriers perceived by students, for example the academic language used.

Approach Two

The second approach was to use previous examination questions (including those in the Additional Study sheet) as a means of recapping on either a particular session or a group of sessions. For example, in the middle of the module groups of 5 or so students were formed. Each group was given a list of 6 questions largely based on the areas covered by the lectures previously and took turns to select a question. All the groups then had 10 minutes to prepare an essay plan. Each essay plan was summarised on a white board and individuals could comment on the differences in approach by each group in terms of structure and content. The module tutor would then comment overall on elements of good or poor practice. This activity enables students to 'learn by doing' in terms of structuring an examination essay and exchange ideas with other students regarding the content required.

Results

Students have consistently commented on module evaluation forms that the additional study sheets used in Approach One are really useful tools when it comes to revision. They are able to compare their lecture notes with the learning outcomes for the session(s) and then supplement this with wider reading. Some students attempt the old examination questions but only one or two pass these on to the module tutor for feedback.

Students also welcome Approach Two as this raises a number of issues relating to structure and content of essay responses to examination questions. Frequently asked questions include; 'What is the difference between 'Evaluate', 'Examine' and 'Assess'?' and 'How should I respond to a question asking me to 'discuss this statement'?'. The benefit of a group approach to looking at examination questions is that, like cryptic crossword clues, they become more achievable and each person tends to have something to contribute.

Impact on overall module performance

A comparison of the 'results' over the last five years shows two changes. First, the overall performance at examinations has improved. When I took over the module there was a history of the examination mark being about 10% lower than that of the coursework. In the last five years the difference has been reduced to less than 5% and in one year it was 0.2% higher. The second element is that the number of students who are performing better in their examination than their coursework is also increasing. Thus in three out of the five years the number of students who have a 5% difference in performance between the two elements of assessment is equally balanced between better performance in the coursework and the better performance in examination.

References

Short, C. (1999) 'Techniques for improving student preparation for examinations', *Journal of Learning and Teaching* *5*(1), 9-11

Short C. (1999) 'Techniques for improving student preparation for examinations', *Geography Discipline Network*, <http://www.glos.ac.uk/gdn/abstracts/a102.htm>

Keywords: examination preparation; examination performance;
             independent study; student handouts

Contact: Christopher Short, School of Environment, University of
             Gloucestershire; 01242 543319; cshort@glos.ac.uk

Appendix D4.1

Multi-Functional Aspects of Land Management & Common Land

Week 5 Additional Study
Learning Outcomes - by the end of the Week 5 lecture and appropriate additional study you should be able to:
- appreciate the context behind countryside change and the move away from production orientated agriculture;
- identify the main attractions of rural areas to non-rural individuals and organisations as well as the changes which have led to rural areas being on an equal footing to towns and cities;
- understand what is meant by the terms: post-productivism; consumerism; and commodification;
- understand what constitutes common land and why it is an example of multi-functional land;
- appreciate the issues involved in managing an area example of multi-functional land where different interests have different objectives.

Example exam questions
1. Indicate and examine the main changes that have occurred during the transition of land use from a production based agriculture to consumerism and commodity based rural enterprises.
2. Define common land and indicate why it is an example of multi-functional land use.

Additional Study
1. Have a look at the Good Practice Guide taking special note of the examples and note the range of objectives relating to the various interests.
2. Read Part III of Rural Politics and/or the introductory chapters of 'Constructing the Countryside' and/or Chapter 2/3 or 4/5 or 6/7 of Jules Pretty's 'Living Land'.

3. Read the full version of one of the four articles listed with their abstract on the attached sheet (Banks and Marsden, 2000; Evans *et al.*, 2002; Marsden, 1999; Oliver and Jenkins, 2003).

References

Countryside and Community Research Unit (1998) *Good Practice Guide on the management of Common Land,* London: DETR

Banks J. and Marsden T. (2000) 'Integrating agri-environment policies, farming systems and rural development: Tir Cymen in Wales' *Sociologia Ruralis, 40* (4), 466-480

Evans N., Morris C. and Winter M. (2002) 'Conceptualizing agriculture: A critique of post-productivism as the new orthodoxy', *Progress in Human Geography, 26* (3), 313-332

Marsden T. (1999) 'Rural futures: The consumption countryside and its regulation', *Sociologia Ruralis, 39* (4), 501-520

Marsden T., Murdoch J., Lowe P., Munton R. and Flynn A. (1993) *Constructing the Countryside,* London: UCL Press. Chaps 1&2

Oliver T. and Jenkins T. (2003) 'Sustaining rural landscapes: The role of integrated tourism' *Landscape Research, 28* (3), 293-307

Pretty, J. (1998) *The Living Land,* London: Earthscan

Short, C. and Winter M. (1999) 'The Problem of Common Land: towards stakeholder governance', *Journal of Environmental Planning and Management 42* (5) 613-630

Short C. (2000) 'Common Land and ELMS: a need for policy innovation in England & Wales', *Land Use Policy, 17,* 121-133

Winter M. (1996) *Rural Politics: policies for agriculture, forestry & the environment,* London: Routledge Part III

D5. Improving examination performance through active engagement of students in a mid-semester peer assessment workshop

Mick Healey and Tim Hall

What is the problem?

Two common observations about examinations are that many students perform poorly and most obtain lower marks in them than they do in the coursework component of the module. A frequent attempt to address this issue is to run revision sessions and emphasise the kinds of things we are looking for in examination answers. However, anecdotal evidence suggests that many students seem not to apply this advice.

What was the response?

This exercise attempts to make a contribution to tackling these issues directly by:

a) encouraging students to take ownership of the issues through getting them to participate and reflect upon the assessment and feedback process; and

b) running the workshop part way through the semester, when there is still time for them to take on board some of the lessons, such as the need for wider reading.

Which students participated?

19 out of 24 students from a Level 2 module, *EL122 Economic Change and Location,* participated.

How did the workshop run?

The students were asked to read the references from the session in week 3 on farm diversification and prepare an essay plan on the following question taken from a previous examination paper: 'The nature of farm diversification varies spatially'. Discuss the geography of farm diversification in the UK with reference to examples.

The following week's session was run as a workshop with the instructions displayed on overhead transparencies:

1. In pairs compare your essay plans. Identify the strengths and weaknesses of each plan.
2. Individually look at the School of Environment assessment grade criteria. Use them to assess the essays written by two students who answered this question in the examination (slightly modified, typed and anonymised). Identify the strengths and weaknesses of the essays and give them a mark out of 100%.
3. In pairs compare the strengths and weaknesses of the two essays and the grades awarded and draft a feedback comments sheet.
4. In plenary list the strengths and weaknesses of each essay.
5. Individually compare your feedback with that of the tutors. Drawing on the workshop discussion make a list of the ways in which you could improve your essay plan.
6. In plenary list the main lessons you will take away from this session.

Only after the plenary in stage 4 did we give the students our own written feedback comments and marks on the two essays. One or more of the pairs in the plenary picked up most of the strengths and weaknesses we had identified. The group marks were more polarised than ours. The students gave the weaker essay, which we had graded as a marginal third/2.2 answer, an average of 43%; whereas they gave the other script, which we awarded a low to mid-2.1 mark, an average of 68%.

What are the benefits of the workshop?
Although the group size was small the mean examination mark the students obtained at the end of semester was identical at 57% to what they obtained in coursework. This compared with a difference of 8 percentage points in the marks the previous cohort obtained (47%

examination and 55% coursework). This finding, though tentative, would seem to support findings from Oxford Brookes, which, on a first year Business Studies module taken by about 500 students, found that participants at a 90 minute workshop on 'active engagement with assessment criteria' performed on average about 6 percentage points better than non-participants (Price *et al* 2002). Prior to the intervention at Brookes there was no significant difference in the marks obtained by the participants and non-participants on a related comparison module.

The main lessons of the peer assessment workshop that the students identified in the final plenary suggest that, if acted upon, these students may perform better than they would have otherwise done in the module examination. Furthermore, because the lessons are largely generic, this improvement may possibly spill over into their performance in examinations in other modules assessed by essays (Table 1).

Table 1: Lessons the students identified they would take away from the workshop

Importance of:
- Developing essay plans, both as part of the revision process and in the examination
- Structuring the answer around the phrasing of the question
- Having a clear explicit structure in the main body of the essay
- Answering who?, what?, when?, why?, and where?
- Incorporating wider reading in answers and not relying solely on lecture notes
- Including evidence (e.g. statistics, facts) and case studies
- Referring to references (by author's name and date) in answers
- Summarising and concluding the answer to the question in terms of the phrasing of the question

What other issues arise from the workshop?

The main disadvantage of holding the workshop is that we had one fewer session out of 12 to present the module. However, the students should have gained a deeper understanding of the topic under discussion (farm diversification) and by actively involving them in the assessment process they should have enhanced their skills in answering examination essay questions.

Evaluation

At the end of module evaluation, all responses praised this initiative. For example:

'It was certainly the most informative lecture I have received in terms of exam preparation. From this lecture I have prepared my revision notes in a different format than I would have previously done. Critically analysing past papers gave me greater knowledge of how to approach questions in exam conditions'.

'Very useful and allowed us to gain a better understanding of what it takes to get a good grade'.

References

Price, M., Rust, C., and O'Donovan, B. (2002) 'Minor interventions can have major effects on student learning from a three year study', *10th International Symposium on Improving Student Learning Theory and Practice – 10 Years On*, Brussels, 4-6 September

Key words: Peer assessment; examination performance; feedback; reflection

Contacts: Mick Healey, School of Environment, University of Gloucestershire; 01242 543364; mhealey@glos.ac.uk

Tim Hall, School of Environment, University of Gloucestershire; 01242 532836; thall@glos.ac.uk

D6. Student module evaluation using a participatory technique

James Garo Derounian

The prompt

The initial prompt was to undertake a mid-semester module evaluation by, with and for, undergraduate students. This was intended as a formative evaluation, to influence the form and content of remaining lecture sessions. It comprised a 30-minute participatory evaluation (using 'stick it' notes), during one lecture class, plus subsequent reflection by the tutor, and report back to students in the light of their suggestions (face to face and *via* a virtual learning environment (WebCT)).

The purpose

This student evaluation, undertaken at the mid-module point, required students to practise the module title/learning outcomes *viz Participation and Consultation*, a Level III module. It also celebrated the use of a participatory technique (to evaluate module delivery/content) and thereby influenced content/delivery of the remaining sessions. The process fostered reflection by both staff and students related to the teaching, learning and assessments for the course. Students undertook 'learning by doing' and gained feedback on how their learning was going – factors 3 & 4 set down by Race (2001, chapter 1). Knowledge and understanding of how to practise the 'Open Space' (community development) participatory technique was adapted to encourage student feedback and comments.

How practices were changed

Changes made in response to student comments included some additional weekly contact sessions (rather than face-to-face interaction on alternate weeks); trying out more participatory techniques in class, as a result of the 'taster' experienced in undertaking the mid module evaluation; clarifying readings/resources relevant to each (remaining) session, and continuing active engagement/learning, in the form of question/answer seminar sessions; reflection on guided readings for student tutorial input and so on.

Gains

- An 'appropriately different' approach to evaluation and adjusting teaching/learning.
- An attempt to tailor the (evaluation) activity to the theme and core of the module (participation/consultation).
- Leaving/trusting students to contribute without direct supervision.
- Learning about aspects of consultation and participation (inclusion, negotiation, partnership etc) through the vehicle of a teaching evaluation.

Students enjoyed evaluating the module by using a novel mechanism other than 'yet another standard evaluation form.' Although geared to a community development module, the technique offers an active, group-based, informal means of students undertaking a mid- or terminal module evaluation.

(Potential) losses

Uncertainty over how many students actually committed suggestions to paper. There is a danger that only the articulate, keen and motivated participate, or that the dominant subvert the group view (but this in itself is another reflection in the spirit of the module content, related to the theory and practice of participation and consultation in decision-making).

References

New Economics Foundation (1998) *Participation works!,* London: NEF

Race, P. (2001) *The lecturer's toolkit: A resource for developing learning, teaching and assessment,* 2nd edition, London: Kogan Page

Wates, N. (2000) *The Community planning handbook* London: Earthscan

Keywords: Evaluation; participation; module review; active reflection on learning; learning by doing

Contact: James Garo Derounian, School of Environment,
University of Gloucestershire; 01242-532990;
jderounian@glos.ac.uk